Brathay
inspiring people

KV-338-623

WITHDRAWN

Self-esteem
and youth development

edited by Kaye Richards

YOUTH DEVELOPMENT PAPERS **1**

LIVERPOOL JMU LIBRARY
3 1111 01361 3581

Self-esteem and Youth Development, Youth Development Papers 1.
ISBN 0 - 9529200 - 3 - 4

Editorial matter and selection © Brathay Hall Trust, 2003.
The individual contributions © the respective authors, 2003.

The opinions expressed in the papers are those of the authors and not necessarily those of the Brathay Hall Trust.

Published by Brathay Hall Trust, Ambleside
Edited by Kaye Richards, Brathay Hall Trust
Designed and typeset by Caroline Barrasford, Kendal
Printed by Stramongate Press, Kendal

Contents

Preface

I am very pleased to introduce a new series of Youth Development publications from the Brathay Academy. This series sits alongside our two existing series: Organisation Development Topical Papers and Occasional Research Papers. This range of publications reflects the breadth of Brathay's work in education, youth work and management learning.

At the heart of all Brathay's work – whether with a group of disaffected young people or a corporate board in times of change – is personal development. Our belief is that real change only occurs when people are engaged holistically: in their emotions and spirits as well as in their minds and bodies. It is therefore fitting that the first publication in this new series, which over the years to come will focus on various aspects of young people's development, should examine the role played by the fundamental concept of self-esteem.

This publication arose from a seminar hosted by the Brathay Academy during 2002, in which Professor Nicholas Emler presented for debate a summary of the research – 'Self-esteem: the costs and causes of low self-worth' – he undertook for the Joseph Rowntree Foundation. The main responses from the seminar to this research report are also included here, along with a number of others. I believe that this publication will help to develop our understanding of this complex but important area.

Steve Lenartowicz
Youth Development Director
Head of Academy

Editorial

Esteeming the self – a worthy pursuit?

Kaye Richards

Introduction

There have been many debates and much controversy over recent years in relation to the value placed upon the ideal of having a high level of self-esteem. A lack of self-esteem has been an all too easy explanation for many 'ills' in the world and has led into what has been defined as a "self-esteem industry" (Emler, 2001). What is evident in youth development is that much emphasis is placed upon the enhancement of self-esteem as being a worthy activity. As a result, projects for developing self-esteem have become commonplace across many developmental, educational and social practices involving young people.

One may say that if people feel good about themselves they will find themselves avoiding many displacement behaviours and activities, such as drug and alcohol abuse, disordered eating and criminal activity. This may be a 'common sense' conclusion, yet it does not provide a sufficient rationale for simply adding the goal of raising self-esteem to a list of intervention aims. Noting self-esteem as an expected outcome of any intervention does not necessarily mean adequate attention has been given to understanding what self-esteem means for the specific target group. Even if certain behaviours can be linked to strong feelings of dislike for oneself and a low self-worth it would be naïve to expect these feelings to manifest themselves in identical ways in different client groups. For example, the self-esteem of a woman with an eating disorder would have some different dynamics from the self-esteem of an individual displaying criminal behaviour. This conclusion suggests that we should critically evaluate the theoretical models that underpin a wide range of self-esteem interventions.

A more thoughtful approach to the 'why' and the 'how' of developing self-esteem in young people does not mean that youth development practices should abandon this notion. What it suggests is the need to engage more fully in the study of wider and often more difficult questions. For example, what does it mean for a young person to 'feel' self-esteem? Why do some people feel good about themselves and others not? How does a personal development intervention work towards developing a higher level of self-esteem in an individual with a low self-esteem? Is there a sufficient relationship between a low self-esteem and certain behaviour to warrant interventions aimed at raising self-esteem in order to change the behaviour? How do we know when an individual has gained a sustainable sense of self-worth? What benefits transpire for an individual when he or she gains self-esteem? What benefits transpire for wider society when an individual gains self-esteem? How does a societal agenda for raising self-esteem impact upon a personal agenda for raising self-esteem? How do these conflict with each other? What does the research evidence tell us about the processes and practices of endeavouring to raise self-esteem in young people?

Questions such as those posed above reflect elements of the enquiry made by Nicholas Emler (2001) into the costs and causes of low self-worth. In a review of available research evidence Emler (*ibid.*) examines whether raising self-esteem is 'the magic bullet' which it is often claimed to be. In questioning the assumptions surrounding self-esteem he examines more thoroughly the links between a range of problem behaviours and self-esteem. As these problem behaviours are central to work with young people the conclusions drawn by Emler encourage those who work in youth development to consider these findings more fully in relation to current practice and policy. A collection of responses to the conclusions made by Emler's report is, therefore, presented here. The aim of these papers is not to provide one simple answer as to whether doubt should be given to all interventions used in work with young people that raise self-esteem. Instead, its aim is to place ideas and thinking, whether these are the ideas and thinking of the researcher or practitioner, into a shared forum. In doing so, it maps out some of the emerging debate that has been initiated as a result of the research report by Emler.

Overview of contributions

Nicholas Emler provides an overview of the main conclusions of his research report on self-esteem, providing details of research evidence currently available and considers measurements of self-esteem. He examines the role of self-esteem in relation to a range of behaviours. These include delinquency, race prejudice, abuse of illegal drugs, alcohol abuse, risky sexual behaviour, susceptibility to social pressure, educational underachievement, eating disorders and suicidal thoughts and actions. He then considers some of the possible sources of low self-esteem; discussing social identities, individual assets and personal influences. Finally, he goes on to consider why any of the issues debated "matter at all" for youth development.

John Huskins introduces a youth work agenda as he relates self-esteem to a holistic perspective of youth work practice. Here he provides an overview of some of the key points made by Emler in his research report and then goes on to consider a model of working with disaffected young people. In providing detail of the process of working with disaffected young people, Huskins enables the youth work agenda to be contextualised more fully.

Frances Walker and Mason Minnitt examine strategies that support the development of self-esteem in young people in the context of an educational agenda. They give detail of how Barrow Community Learning Partnership – an Education Action Zone – places self-esteem as part of a wider educational process. However, they note that self-esteem development is an integrated process of developing social and emotional skills. As a result they highlight that in enabling young people to feel good about themselves what is required is a developmental process of identifying their various 'gifts and talents'.

Jennifer Peel examines the ways in which a theoretical understanding of a Person-Centred approach to personal development can help to highlight the ways in which motivational tendencies can impact upon how a person experiences his or her self-worth. She describes the ways in which the Actualising Tendency of an individual can easily be drowned out by a person's search for conditional acceptance. In order to reverse such a self-defeating process she highlights how the core conditions – as drawn from a Person-Centred perspective – of warmth, empathy and congruence enable an individual to move away from self-doubt to a more non-judgmental experience of their core sense of self. This account exemplifies how theory guides practical approaches to working with young people.

Alison Butcher shares insights from her practice as a youth development trainer. She points out some of the transitional processes faced by young people as they negotiate the move towards adulthood, noting the ways in which these processes can impact upon how young people experience themselves. As a way of giving them a voice she recalls two examples of working with young people. Here she moves away from a theoretical analysis, as provided in other papers, into her professional experience of trying to impact upon how young people view themselves in the world. As she unravels some elements of young people's journeys she brings into focus many of the processes youth workers are faced with on a daily basis as they try to understand what they might mean about self-esteem in their practice.

Steve Lenartowicz offers a brief overview of youth work policy and practice. In providing this, he encourages the wider self-esteem debate to consider how aspects of this can be related to and situated within the national priorities for policies that affect young people's education and development: for example, social inclusion, citizenship and employability. Using the example of self-esteem, he highlights how an uncritical approach to youth work easily leaves its practices open to criticism.

Barbara Smith provides an account of how she approaches her work with young people by having 'no strings attached' to the outcomes. Instead, she focuses upon relational opportunities in order to assist the personal growth of young people. Drawing upon the concept of 'strokes' and 'stroke economy' from Transactional Analysis Psychotherapy, she provides an example of specific strategies that can be used when working with young people. She illustrates some of the minutiae of the processes of 'stroking' by sharing a short case study of working with a young boy – Sam. This case study is illustrative of the need for theoretically-guided interventions in enabling young people to develop a stronger and more durable sense of self-worth.

Peter Bunyan gives attention to the tension that easily emerges when theory is related to practice. In acknowledging this tension he then goes on to discuss some key theoretical positions in relation to self-esteem. Interwoven with such accounts is an evaluation of some implications for practice. For example, he describes self-worth protection strategies which people can display when they experience a threat to their sense of self-worth. He also raises critical questions to the reality of practices of raising self-esteem, recognising that a person's self-esteem is in fact resilient to change.

Finally, my own contribution considers theory and practice with a client group that is central to debates on self-esteem and young people – young women with eating disorders. It is an account of how theory has directly informed practice in the development of an intervention for women with eating disorders. This example places a strong emphasis on 'relational psychology' as a component of working with young women's self-esteem. Also, questioning the ways in which the outdoors is often used as a vehicle for the raising of self-esteem illustrates how a more analytical approach to working with self-esteem enhancement with young people is required.

Conclusion

The common use of the term self-esteem and its enhancement has, perhaps, provided a strategy for bypassing some challenging questions about the processes of working with young people. This is not surprising, given that understanding the self and its development is an endeavour that continues to puzzle many of us. However, questioning the grand narrative of self-esteem invites us to ask what factors enable an individual to attain a sense of identity that avails itself to fully expressing his or her capabilities and associated qualities – 'gifts and talents' – in the world.

Telling someone they 'should' and 'could' feel good doesn't go very far towards making them feel good about who and what they are. The processes of unravelling the extent to which an individual holds feelings of self-hate towards themselves and then reversing such feelings into self-like is not necessarily a 'happy' process of change – it deals with many feelings, anxieties, and tensions. Thus, developing a sustainable sense of self-worth requires more than a 'quick fix' approach. Many interventions may support the journey towards encouraging a durable sense of self-esteem in young people. However, as discussed in the papers presented here, many interventions would benefit from linking more thoroughly theories of self-esteem development with facilitation of psychological change to ascertain clearly what role it plays – if any – in the long-term task of raising self-esteem.

LIVERPOOL JOHN MOORES UNIVERSITY
LEARNING SERVICES

Although a somewhat fragmented debate at times, it is clear that the self-esteem debate bridges a recognised gap between research, theory and practice in youth development. A dynamic relationship between all these three areas needs to be fostered in developing 'on the ground' youth work. Research is necessary to help question and assess what is done in practice. Theory is needed to help support and guide practice. Practice is needed to understand what is meant by self-esteem enhancement in action. It is important that ongoing dialogue is achieved between all parties involved. Whether it is the practitioners working with young people on a daily basis, or the researchers and theoreticians trying to examine the dimensions and assess the effectiveness of interventions, all of us who work with issues relevant to young people have something to offer to this ongoing debate.

In conclusion, it could be argued that the journey towards self-esteem is the development of a self-identity that enables an individual to internally accept him or herself in the light of all the possibilities and limitations of being a human being. We all stand on the threshold of our capacity to embrace a healthy and loving sense of self. Yet, the question remains as to what role does youth work have in enabling all young people to access such a threshold? Further, how can a more honest and open questioning of the 'why' and 'how' of self-esteem enhancement enable young people to be able to step across this threshold if this is an endeavour that youth development practices continue to pursue in forthcoming years?

References

Emler, N. (2001). *Self-esteem: The costs and causes of low self-worth.* York: Joseph Rowntree Foundation YPS.

Does it really matter if some young people have low self-esteem?

Nicholas Emler

Introduction

Lack of self-esteem we have been told by Oprah Winfrey (Harrison, 1989: 29) "is the root of all the problems in the world" and certain more scientifically qualified authorities barely disagree. According to Smelser (1989), diminished self-esteem is a powerful independent cause in the genesis of major social problems. In contrast, high self-esteem has been described as a potent "social vaccine" (California Task Force to Promote Self Esteem, 1990), offering immunity against these same ills. It has even been likened to a magic bullet; the key to teenagers' futures (Katz, 2000). It is barely surprising, therefore, that the promotion of self-esteem has become a major business enterprise. The purpose of this article is to caution against the goods this enterprise offers; they are unlikely to be what we need most, and very unlikely to deliver the benefits promised.

My thesis, put simply, is that low self-esteem is not the explanation, and not even part of the explanation, for most of the negative consequences attributed to it. In fact there are only a few costs of low self-esteem, mostly borne by the individual so afflicted and not by society at large. I will also, however, have something to say about the sources of self-esteem and will conclude that many of the conditions previously assumed to diminish it do not in fact have this effect. I will refer briefly to the effectiveness of interventions intended to raise self-esteem, asking also whether they are worth the effort.

As to what motivates me to make this argument, there are two principle considerations. First, I believe we owe ourselves honesty; human welfare and prosperity never have been much advanced by believing things that are not true. However, the point could still be made that a belief in the benefits of high self-esteem even, if seriously overstated, is largely benign. This brings me to my second consideration: this belief is not benign. On the contrary, it has done real damage.

The next thing a reader is entitled to ask is what warrant I have for the argument offered. My response is that I do not expect you simply to accept a personal opinion. Your task would be easier if you were prepared to accept my judgment as a research scientist, but ultimately I would rather you were persuaded by the evidence. Unfortunately, this requires some work on your part; the relevant evidence is not easily interpreted or easily understood. I emphasise this in particular because the subject can produce strong passions, not least among those who disagree with the conclusions I draw. But I am also passionate about this and passionate in particular about the need to take account of, comprehend, and evaluate evidence appropriately. In the end there is no other intellectually or morally defensible way to settle the argument.

This article is not a comprehensive presentation of this evidence. Instead it describes the principal conclusions of a report I prepared for the Joseph Rowntree Foundation (Emler, 2001). That report identifies and describes the relevant research evidence in more detail. Ideally, nonetheless, you would read the original published research reports themselves. But I also recognise this may not for many good reasons be a realistic option for readers of this article, and so I owe you my honest assessment of what the evidence tells us.

The best research evidence currently available

If practice in working with young people is to be guided by the best research evidence currently available, how do we decide what is 'the best research evidence'? In the case of self-esteem, its effects and its origins, an immense amount of research has already been published. It is currently running in the region of a thousand newly published studies each year. So it should, in principle, be possible to find in this body of findings, clear answers to all the questions we might have. Unfortunately, however, the research is of variable quality; some studies are more informative than others.

The most informative will be based on a research design that can answer causal questions, which is to say questions of the following kind:

does low self esteem lead to greater involvement in delinquency? Merely observing that, for example, young people involved in delinquency have lower self-esteem than those who are not, is insufficient; it tells us nothing about what is cause and what is effect in this observed association.

In psychology, as in other sciences, the best option for answering causal questions is the experiment, and many experimental studies have indeed been carried out in this area. However, this option has two disadvantages. First, an experiment can demonstrate the effects of lowering self-esteem, not the effects of having low self-esteem. We have no grounds for assuming the former are equivalent to the latter, and plenty of reasons to suspect that they are not. Second, an experimental manipulation that permanently depressed a person's self-esteem would undoubtedly be unethical.

The more realistic option, avoiding both problems, is the prospective longitudinal study. In such a study one might assess the self-esteem of a sample of young people on one occasion and then return to the same people on later occasions, perhaps once a year for several years, assess their self-esteem again and assess any pattern of behaviour or outcome – such as pregnancy or suicide attempts – that one suspects of being influenced by self-esteem. For various reasons this solution is not perfect, but if, to pursue these examples, one discovered that those who had lower self-esteem on the first occasion they were studied were more likely at some later point in time to have made a suicide attempt or to have become pregnant, this would increase one's confidence that low self-esteem was in some part responsible for these outcomes.

Confidence in this or other conclusions is further increased if the design of the research is not only longitudinal but also multivariate; that is, the design should include the assessment of as many as possible of the variables that are potentially related to the outcomes of interest. So, for example, young females with poor academic abilities may as a result be more at risk of teenage pregnancy and young people in general with such deficits may, as a result, be more inclined to make suicide attempts. In both cases they may, again as a result of their poor academic abilities, have lower self-esteem. If self-esteem alone had been assessed and not also academic abilities, it would not be possible to decide on this alternative explanation. A multivariate design in which several potential causal influences are assessed, and moreover are assessed at several points in time, allows one to consider and potentially to rule out a larger number of alternative possibilities of these kinds.

A third quality of good evidence is that it will be based upon a large and representative sample. The more representative the sample of the population as a whole the more confident one can be that any conclusions apply to the population as a whole – in the case of teenage pregnancy risks, all teenage girls – and not just to some small sub-set of the population – e.g. white, working class girls. It is more difficult for small samples to be representative in this way.

A large sample has the additional benefit of allowing one to decide not only whether, given that the research design is in other respects appropriate, a causal association exists, but how strong this association is. It is highly unlikely that low self-esteem is the only risk factor for any outcome of interest. If it is implicated at all it will be one of several risk factors. Decisions about effective intervention need to be based on evidence of the relative importance of different risk factors. If, for example, low self-esteem proved to be the least consequential of six risk factors for drug abuse, one might reasonably decide that intervention efforts should focus on one or more of the other six.

At this point I must reveal there is both good news and bad news. The bad news is that despite the massive research output very little of it meets all three standards – longitudinal, multivariate, and large scale. The good news is that enough research does now approximate to these standards to allow some reasonably unequivocal conclusions about at least some of the questions of interest. Before turning to this we need to consider one further vital piece of the jigsaw; the measurement of self-esteem.

What is self-esteem and how can it be measured?

Measurement requires an agreed definition. The definition most widely used by researchers is that self-esteem is an attitude varying from positive to negative (Rosenberg, 1965). From this point, however, agreement has not been perfect. One approach, Rosenberg's, has been to treat this attitude as essentially an emotional response expressed, in the case of high self-esteem, as liking, respecting, admiring and approving of oneself. Another treats it as, at base, an intellectual appraisal of the self, a judgment and summing up of one's various assets and liabilities. Thus, Stanley Coopersmith's (1967: 4) widely cited definition refers to "the extent to which the individual believes himself to be capable, significant, successful and worthy". Such beliefs are supposedly arrived at by evaluating oneself against various criteria of excellence. The difference in emphasis in these two approaches – one stressing the emotional response as basic, the other the cognitive response – have some non-trivial implications, as we shall see. The practical consequences, however, are less significant. Each provides a basis for constructing measures of self-esteem that have reasonable precision but the resulting measurement procedures produce similar results (Blaskovich & Tomaka, 1991).

Consequences of low self-esteem

What do we know about the consequences of low self-esteem and with what degree of certainty? In what follows, I have chosen consequences with respect to which sufficient good evidence now exists to draw some conclusions. These consequences are: delinquency, racism, drug abuse, alcohol abuse, risky sexual behaviour, susceptibility to peer pressure, educational attainment, eating disorders, and suicidal thoughts and actions. This list also has the merit of including many of the current major concerns about young people.

Delinquency

There have been three principle arguments for the role of diminished self-esteem in delinquent and criminal behaviour. One is that, once young people are convinced they are worthless, the risk of being criticised for their conduct ceases to be a deterrent (Scheff *et al.*, 1989). A second links two assumptions about young people and crime; that their criminal behaviour reflects the bad influence of criminal acquaintances and that they are vulnerable to such influences to the extent that their self-esteem is low. The third argument is that young people want to think well of themselves, find it distressing when they do not and therefore seek out opportunities to reduce this distress by doing anything that can make them feel good about themselves (Kaplan, 1980). For some young people, delinquency is one of the few options they have to meet this need for 'esteem enhancement'.

The first two arguments predict a straightforward association between low self-esteem and greater involvement in delinquency. According to the third, however, we should find that young people who initially have the lowest self-esteem will be the most likely to engage in delinquency subsequently, but if they do this their self-esteem should then rise.

Good evidence is available addressing these predictions. At least four separate studies (Bynner *et al.*, 1981; Jang & Thornberry, 1998; McCarthy & Hoge, 1984: Wells & Rankin, 1983) meeting the relevant standards have now shown the following. Young people with low self-esteem are no more, or indeed less, likely than others to become involved in delinquency as a result. Additionally, engaging in delinquency does not enhance self-esteem. On the other hand, however, delinquency does under some circumstances have a small negative effect on self-esteem.

Race prejudice

The most popular case for an influence of self-esteem on race prejudice is based on the theory that people derive a sense of their own worth from the prestige or value of the social groups with which they are identified (e.g., Tajfel, 1978). However, the value of these groups can only be determined relatively, which is to say by comparison with other groups to which the individual does not belong. This introduces an incentive to find that one's own group is superior by concluding that others are inferior.

This analysis has given rise to two predictions. First, self-esteem will benefit from opportunities to confirm the superiority of one's own group by discriminating against representatives of others and conversely will suffer when one is denied this opportunity. Second, the tendency to discriminate against others on the basis of the groups to which they belong will be strongest in those with the greatest need to raise their self-esteem, namely those who initially have least. Both predictions have been tested and the first has consistently been supported; the second has not (Rubin & Hewstone, 1998). Indeed, almost all tests of this prediction have confirmed completely the opposite: those most disposed to discriminate are those whose self-esteem is initially the highest (*see* also Aberson *et al.*, 2000).

Abuse of illegal drugs

There are four clear grounds for expecting a causal pathway from low self-esteem to drug abuse. One treats such abuse as criminal, a second treats it as a health risk. Thus, grounds of the first kind are similar to one of the arguments linking low self-esteem to delinquency: if people already have a poor opinion of themselves and, therefore, little more to lose from public condemnation, they will be relatively undeterred from drug abuse by this possibility. According to a second kind of argument, if low self-esteem is a negative attitude towards the self then it implies a readiness to treat the self badly. In other words, drug abuse is abuse of the self if not wilful neglect of the well-being of the self.

The third option has been to attribute drug abuse to negative peer influences. This view has, if anything, been advocated even more strongly here than in the case of delinquency, and has provided the underlying rationale for a number of drug prevention and intervention programmes aimed at young people. The fourth option is another version of the esteem enhancement hypothesis. It emphasises the immediate effect of drug use, namely making the user feel good, at least temporarily. Drug use, therefore, may provide a transitory escape from the misery of low self-esteem.

Each of these accounts predicts a straightforward association between low self-esteem and drug abuse. Some research has shown such an association (e.g., Neumark-Sztainer *et al.*, 1997), some has not (e.g., Laflin *et al.*, 1994); overall, no consistent pattern has emerged. As always the most informative evidence would be provided by prospective longitudinal studies, but in this case there are very few such studies. Only one (Olmstead *et al.*, 1991) has so far shown that low self-esteem can predict later drug abuse. But this particular study also reveals the importance of measuring the supposed outcome – substance abuse in this case – on the first occasion those in the sample are surveyed. It turned out that the strongest predictor of later substance abuse was earlier substance abuse.

One other source of evidence comes from studies evaluating the impact of programmes to raise self-esteem. If low self-esteem leads to drug abuse then this risk should be reduced by raising self-esteem. So far, no carry-over effect of raising self-esteem upon drug abuse has been demonstrated (Hopkins *et al.*, 1988; Stoil *et al.*, 2000). More generally, the only safe conclusion at present is that a causal link between low esteem and drug abuse has not been proven.

Alcohol abuse

A link between alcohol abuse and low self-esteem has been anticipated for what will now be familiar reasons, even if the case is slightly different from that of drug abuse. Alcohol abuse is not illegal, although purchase of alcohol by those under eighteen is of course illegal. Alcohol consumption does not attract a high level of social disapproval, although excessive consumption can do so. Nonetheless it has been anticipated that young people who lack self-esteem will be vulnerable to alcohol abuse because they have little further to lose from any consequent disapproval. In so far as alcohol abuse is understood to damage health, then it would seem to constitute abuse of the self. The esteem enhancement argument can also be applied here, assuming that the primary motivation of alcohol abusers is the temporary euphoria achieved, if not the similarly short-lived escape from more lucid self-awareness.

Research on the self-esteem of diagnosed alcoholics is very clear in its conclusions: such people do have lower self-esteem than non-alcoholics (Skager & Kerst, 1989). However, this very consistent pattern is also consonant with the view that low self-esteem is the consequence not the cause. Several longitudinal studies have revealed no association between earlier self-esteem and later levels of alcohol use (McGee & Williams, 2000; Newcomb *et al.*, 1986; Silbereisen *et al.*, 1990; Winefield *et al.*, 1989); the only exception to this is one study (Scheier *et al.*, 2000) indicating that adolescents with low self-esteem were less likely to increase their alcohol consumption subsequently than those who had higher self-esteem.

Risky sexual behaviour

The risks here are various, but central among them are the risks to health of sexually transmitted disease and the risk for girls of pregnancy in their teenage years. The risky patterns of behaviour at issue are, therefore, early and frequent intercourse, unprotected intercourse and intercourse with multiple partners.

Let us first acknowledge that low self-esteem does emerge as a clear risk factor for teenage pregnancy (Herrenkohl *et al.*, 1998; Kaplan *et al.*, 1979; McCauley, 1995; Plotnick & Butler, 1991; Robbins *et al.*, 1985). The question we now have to address is why this is so, and in particular whether it is because low self-esteem increases the likelihood of one or more of the above patterns of behaviour. Taking first early and frequent intercourse, these patterns are not associated with low self-esteem (Cvetkovich & Grote, 1980; McGee & Williams, 2000; West & Sweeting, 1997). The picture for number of partners is similar and also for contraceptive use; in each case no consistent association with self-esteem has been identified (Cvetkovich & Grote, 1980; Garris, *et al.*, 1976; McCorquodale & DeLamater, 1978; McNair *et al.*, 1998).

This leaves something of a puzzle. The greater risk of pregnancy among teenage girls with low self-esteem must arise because they have more unprotected intercourse than those with high self-esteem. However, no general tendency towards more limited and ineffective contraceptive measures has been shown for teenagers in this category. Is pregnancy, therefore, as some have suggested (e.g., Luker, 1975), a calculated choice, rather than an unintended and unplanned side effect of a risky behaviour pattern? Or is it a form of victimisation, in which the victim's choice has been pre-empted at some point by a partner? This is one area in which appropriately targeted research would most certainly be helpful.

Susceptibility to social pressure

One argument commonly made for young people's vulnerability – whether to involvement in criminal activities, drug or alcohol abuse, smoking or risky sexual behaviour – is that their vulnerability is increased by their inability to resist peer pressure. Thus, health campaigners will often advocate interventions intended to increase the capacity of young people to resist these pressures and will almost as often regard raising self-esteem as the appropriate means to this end. But does low self-esteem in reality create greater susceptibility to influence and conformity pressures?

Considerable research attention has been devoted to this question, to the extent that we now have the beginnings of a clear answer (Rhodes & Wood, 1992). There is an association between self-esteem and both conformity and persuadeability. It is people, however, with moderate, rather than low or high self-esteem who show the greatest inclination to be influenced or to conform to the behaviour of others. This is not yet a decisive answer because so little of the relevant research has involved young people, and very little has explored the influence of friends and acquaintances as opposed to relative strangers. Again, more focussed research would be helpful here.

Perhaps, we also need to revisit our assumptions about social influence. These have tended to emphasise only the downside of others' influences. A more reasonable position, I submit, is that it is healthy and adaptive to take into account the opinions of others when deciding how one should behave. If young people do show an inclination to go along with their peers this is more often than not a force for good (cf. Emler & Reicher, 1995). The problem individuals are not those enmeshed in a broad web of interpersonal influences but those whose relative social isolation leaves them dependent on just a few sources of influence.

Educational underachievement

No single aspect of self-esteem has attracted quite so much research attention as its relation to education. This may be because educational outcomes are themselves linked to so many other aspects of young people's lives. Those who leave education the earliest and with the fewest qualifications are also those particularly at risk for delinquency, drug abuse, racially motivated violence against others and, for girls, teenage pregnancy. This has raised the expectation that low self-esteem is so damaging for young people because it erodes their chances of academic success. But do children do more poorly in school because their self-esteem is low?

The large amount of research directed to this question paints a consistent picture. Self-esteem and educational attainment are related, but not strongly related (Hansford & Hattie, 1982; West *et al.*, 1980). Moreover, most of this is due to an effect of attainment on self-esteem (Hoge *et al.*, 1995). In contrast, earlier self-esteem has only a trivial effect on later educational attainment (Feinstein, 2000). However, the findings regarding social influence may also be relevant here. Teaching and learning entail an influence relationship, and we have seen that those with high and with low self-esteem are relatively insensitive to influence. It may be that so far as learning is concerned the optimal level of self-esteem is moderate.

Eating disorders

The most popular reason to have been advanced thus far for an association between self-esteem and eating disorders is that these latter conditions characterise individuals who are unhappy with something about themselves, typically their body shape or weight or appearance. Another interpretation treats eating disorders as forms of self-abuse.

Here again research does indicate a link. Low self-esteem is associated with a range of eating disorders including anorexia, bulimia and unhealthy weight loss (e.g., Neumark-Sztainer *et al.*, Rabe, 1996; Ross & Ivis, 1999; Shisslak *et al.*, 1995; Willcox & Sattler, 1996; Williams *et al.*, 1993). However, the evidence that prior low self-esteem increases the likelihood of developing an eating disorder subsequently is less consistent (see Button *et al.*, 1996; Calam & Waller, 1998; McGee & Williams, 2000; Wood *et al.*, 1994). The safest conclusion on the basis of present knowledge is that self-esteem has an influence, but it is one among several influences, certainly not the strongest (cf. Veron-Guidry *et al.*, 1997), and quite possibly interacts in complex ways with other risk factors (Waller, 2001).

Suicidal thoughts and actions

Fortunately very few young people successfully complete suicide attempts – maybe one in 10,000 in any one year. Suicide as such, therefore, is not a problem on the scale of delinquency or drug abuse. Yet, suicidal thoughts and suicide attempts are relatively more common phenomena, and from what we have learned so far about self-esteem and its consequences it would be a surprise if low self-esteem was quite unrelated to these phenomena. The relevant research has not produced any such surprise (for suicidal thoughts, see e.g., De Man *et al.*, 1992; Marciano & Kazdin, 1994; van Gastel *et al.*, 1997; Vella *et al.*, 1996.

For suicide attempts, see e.g., Boudewyn & Liem, 1995; Overholser *et al.*, 1995; Petrie *et al.*, 1988. For completed suicides, see Kjelsberg *et al.*, 1994).

It does not follow, however, that low self-esteem by itself provides the explanation for suicidal thoughts and actions. There are several risk factors for these outcomes, including family breakdown, alcohol and drug abuse, experience of sexual abuse, and feelings of loneliness (Garnefski, *et al.*, 1992; Kienhosrt *et al.*, 1990; Kjelsberg *et al.*, 1994). Moreover, the effects of these are independent of any effect of low self-esteem. We also need to recognise that very low self-esteem partly overlaps with depression (Kingsbury *et al.*, 1999). Discovering that young people who contemplate, attempt or manage suicide have been depressed is not discovering a great deal.

Summarising the consequences of low self-esteem

Low self-esteem has few negative effects that have been clearly demonstrated. Thus there are no grounds for expecting that young people with low self-esteem will, as a result, be more involved in delinquency, more inclined to support or express racist sentiments, or more at risk of alcohol abuse. There may be a very slightly increased risk of drug abuse or failure in school. Low self-esteem does, however, increase the risk of teenage pregnancy and of suicidal thoughts and actions, and it may play a role in the development of eating disorders. However, in each of these latter cases self-esteem is only one of a number of risk factors.

The picture might be summed up by saying that young people with low self-esteem may be more liable to harm themselves, but not to harm others. This is also consistent with the rather limited evidence available so far on victimisation. Youngsters with low self-esteem have an increased risk of being victims (Egan & Perry, 1998; Hawker & Boulton, 2000); it is as if their low opinion of themselves also invites maltreatment by others.

What of the sources of self-esteem?

Despite the limited consequences of low self-esteem there may still be a case for trying to raise it. But in that case we need first to understand what, in the normal course of events, damages or lowers a young person's sense of their own worth and what protects or enhances it. The candidates for these effects can be grouped into three kinds, social identities, individual assets and personal influences.

Social identities

The idea that our sense of worth is derived from the social categories to which we belong has been, as we have seen, strongly promoted, particularly within psychology. More specific claims have been made about the effects of belonging to categories defined by race, socio-economic status, and gender, in each case by virtue of the relative prestige of the categories concerned. Nonetheless, the self esteem of, for example, young black people or young people with a working class background is no lower than that of young people in apparently more privileged and prestigious social categories (Gray-Little & Hafdahl, 2000; Rosenberg & Perlin, 1978; Wiltfang & Scarbecz, 1990). In the case of black youngsters the evidence very clearly indicates the reverse (Gray-Little & Hafdahl, 2000). Nor is there any tendency for self-esteem to be damaged by membership of a stigmatised category (Croker & Major, 1989).

In the case of gender there is a small difference; girls on average have lower scores on measures of self-esteem than boys and this difference is largest in late adolescence (Kling *et al.*, 1999). Precisely why this difference should occur and should be most marked at this age is unclear. Several explanations have been advanced but so far none has convincingly been either supported or ruled out.

Individual assets

Part of our common sense about self-esteem is that it is based on the judgments each of us makes about our own assets, and this is directly reflected in many of the procedures to measure self-esteem. If we think ourselves more attractive, competent, likeable, virtuous and successful, then we will think better of ourselves in general. But this begs a tricky question about the reliability of our judgments: are these assessments accurate?

How young people feel about their appearance turns out to be strongly correlated with their self-esteem (Harter, 1998). But their own estimates of their appearance are only tenuously related to the judgments that detached observers make (e.g., Kostanski & Gullone, 1998). Self-esteem is similarly closely tied to perceptions of personal successes and failures. Again, however, the self-perceptions are very imperfectly related to any objective assessment of these (Taylor & Brown, 1988). If subjective judgements are unreliable then it makes sense that feedback from others should inform our judgments about ourselves. Yet again, however, what people claim they know about others' judgements are only loosely related to the judgments these others make in practice (Kenny, 1994).

One of the most striking things research may have revealed about self-esteem is the powerful influence it exercises over the way we see ourselves (Borhnstedt & Felson, 1983) and in particular the way it preserves these perceptions in the face of conflicting evidence. First, therefore, self-esteem appears to underlie and influence the estimates we make of our various assets and liabilities rather than to reflect or be derived from them. So, for example, young people will conclude they are physically unattractive because they have low self-esteem rather than suffering a loss of self-esteem because they have decided they are not attractive.

Second, self-esteem protects these perceptions through a variety of psychological defences. Counter evidence is discounted as unreliable, forgotten or not noticed in the first place. Moreover, both high and low self-esteem are defended by such distortions (Taylor & Brown, 1998). So those who lack self-esteem consistently deny there is anything worthy about them, attributing successes to luck or overly lenient examiners, remembering only failures with any accuracy, and expecting the future to be bleak. This helps to explain why real assets and liabilities, real successes and failures are of such limited consequence for self-esteem. But this being so, what is of consequence?

Personal influences

The clearest influences on a young person's self-esteem are his or her parents. As to what matters about parents, the following four factors have proved to be important (cf. Coopersmith, 1967):

- The amount of acceptance, approval and affection shown.
- The degree to which clear standards of conduct are promoted.
- The degree to which discipline is based on explanation rather than force.
- The degree to which children are involved in family decision-making and valued as contributors to the family.

Of these, the qualities of approval and acceptance have particular importance (Feiring & Tasker, 1996). The other side of the coin is that significant damage to self-esteem can be done by physical and particularly sexual abuse in childhood (Kendall-Tackett *et al.*, 1993). Damage to self-esteem is also produced by the absence for whatever reason of one or both parents (Armistead *et al.*, 1995).

Apart from parents, few other relationships in life have quite such an impact upon self-esteem. Nonetheless, it is clear that being loved, accepted, included and shown intimacy by others does benefit the self-esteem of young people, as it does that of adults (e.g., Aron *et al.*, 1995; Stanley & Arora, 1998).

Interventions

There is a massive industry devoted to the promotion of self-esteem, providing everything from self-help literature to training courses and resource centres. This effort has not yet been matched by comparable efforts to evaluate the effects or effectiveness of planned interventions. Nonetheless it is clear that self-esteem can be raised by intervention programmes. This much is clear from the limited evaluations that have been carried out. Moreover, interventions are more effective to the extent that they are based on relevant theory and research evidence (Haney & Durlak, 1998). Beyond these broad conclusions, however, we know very little at all with any certainty. In particular, very little of the evaluation research has yet examined the longer term impact of interventions: are initial gains in self-esteem retained much beyond the end of the intervention, and do such gains have other benefits? One exception is evaluation of programmes to reduce drug abuse by raising self-esteem. No such benefits have yet been demonstrated (e.g., Lynham *et al.*, 2000; Stoil *et al.*, 2000).

Finally, we know next to nothing about the relative cost-effectiveness of these interventions. In the absence of such knowledge we have little sensible basis for allocating resources to tackle the problems young people may face, and certainly none to justify investment in self-esteem.

Why any of this matters at all

There are at least three reasons why we should pay attention to what can be learned from the research evidence on self-esteem and its consequences:

- ***Resources consumed in pursuit of false remedies are resources that cannot then be put to more productive uses:***
  A great deal of time, human ingenuity and money has been invested in, for example, programmes targeted at adolescent drug use and intended to raise young people's self-esteem. It is now clear that these resources could have been put to better use.

- ***Diversion of attention from what actually matters:***
  By focusing on lack of self-esteem as the root cause of so many personal and social ills, we have neglected to consider plausible alternatives. In the case of youthful involvement in crime, for example, there really is no evidence that diminished self-esteem plays a part, but we have very strong clues as to the identity of factors that do matter: poor parenting, a sense of exclusion from the law's protection, lack of realistic employment prospects, for example (Emler & Reicher, 1995).

- ***The destructive distortion of healthy practices:***
  Some of the more zealous and strident promotion of self-esteem has done real damage to people's confidence in dealing with young people (Baumeister, 1998). Thus, parents have become wary of setting clear standards and expectations in case this damages their children's self-esteem. Teachers have developed inhibitions about giving critical feedback or identifying failing performances for similar reasons. Further, it is not helpful to enter adult life with entirely unrealistic views of one's talents because no-one wanted to risk being more honest about one's shortcomings.

Concluding observations

What I hope this article will achieve is openness to the evidence. By this I do not mean that one should accept the conclusions of every published scientific report; on the contrary. There are three questions to ask about any piece of evidence:

1. Does the research design allow one to draw clear conclusions about what is cause and what is effect?
2. How successfully has the research ruled out alternative possible conclusions?
3. How large and representative is the sample upon which the conclusions are based?

If you can find clear answers to these questions you will seldom be led astray by the evidence.

Finally, I wish to say something about seven of the more common, and among them more critical, reactions I have had to the JRF report:

- ***Why should we believe research conclusions if they contradict common sense or professional judgement?*** *"Why should I give up my cherished prejudices?"*

Over the centuries common sense has included many 'truths' that have turned out to be nonsense – that the earth is flat, that some women (witches) had the power of flight (for which they were later murdered in their thousands), or that all women are naturally feeble-minded and incapable of rational thought; that infections and disease are caused by malign spirits, and so on. Common sense has never by itself been a reliable guide to the truth. The more dangerous because more persuasive illusion is that judgment based on professional practice provides a better road to the truth than scientific research. Fair tests of these alternatives have never shown professional judgment to have the advantage.

- ***Why should we believe conclusions based on statistics?*** *"Even damn lies are preferable, given that you can prove anything with statistics."*

This is comforting nonsense, both to those who dislike the conclusions and to those unwilling or unable to understand the argument. Research on persuasion (e.g., Petty & Wegener, 1998) tells us something interesting: you can use weak arguments or even no arguments at all to persuade people of almost anything, but only under certain conditions. If they are already convinced of the opposite, matters will not be so easy. You will then require strong arguments, and even then you may not succeed. In particular, they will remain unpersuaded if they do not pay attention to or understand the argument. Statistics have been more accurately described as principled argument (Abelson, 1995); as such they cannot be used to argue for a lie. The problem, rather, is that they also constitute a demanding and difficult argument. Understandably, therefore, many people do not engage in the argument, and are content to let those they see as more expert fight it out. However, simply to dismiss statistical evidence because it is statistics is not a defensible option.

- ***Why should we accept psychologists' definitions of self-esteem?*** *"This is not what I mean by self-esteem."*

This is fair enough if your own definition helps your practice, but if you also want it to be an alternative to mine then it must pass two tests. It must be capable of translation into procedures for measurement, on which we can all agree. If not, it remains a private fantasy. And the measurement procedure based upon it must produce results different from those produced by mine. Underlying this reaction, however, there is sometimes a deeper aversion. The idea that a quality like self-esteem can be described in numbers at all seems objectionable. My response is that unless this quality can be detected by some objective test, and more specifically unless the test can show whether there is more or less of it, then one can draw no conclusions whatsoever about its causal role in any pattern of behaviour. One most certainly cannot conclude that some intervention has caused self-esteem to rise.

- ***Hasn't the research confused real with false self-esteem?*** *"Aren't a lot of people who claim to have high self-esteem really in denial?"*

In other words, have we simply failed to detect that drug abusers, delinquents, school drop-outs, and bullies in reality have very low self-esteem but have hidden this from us, and perhaps from themselves, with a brave façade? If the difference between true and false self-esteem is so well hidden as to be undetectable, then for all practical purposes it ceases to be a meaningful distinction. The actions of some people may indeed be controlled by invisible aliens, but if we can neither identify these people nor detect the alien presence this proposition lies outside the realm of science.

- ***Is more research really needed here?*** *"Why can't you people come up with clear answers?"*

On the face of it, this is a reasonable complaint. If so much research effort has still not produced clear answers why should anyone believe it will do so in the future? My response is that what we are trying to do here is not rocket science; it is more difficult than that. Human behaviour within the complex interplay of psychological and social forces is an immensely more complex phenomenon than just about anything else addressed by science. Yet our attitudes as a society to social science research remain ambivalent. We seem to want clear answers but we do not want them to cost very much. The sad truth, however, is that cheap research produces cheap answers which are liable to fall apart on close inspection. Good research, research that can provide sound, informative answers, is likely to be expensive. However, with respect to the effects of self-esteem, we can now narrow down the search for profitable areas in which to seek answers. Three clear candidates include teenage pregnancy, eating disorders and openness to influence and persuasion.

- ***If all the claims (or most of them) previously made about self-esteem are untrue, why have these ideas been so popular?*** *"Are you seriously suggesting so many people have been so completely deluded?"*

This is akin to what Richard Dawkins has aptly called the "argument from incredulity": because it defies my beliefs and those of people like me, it cannot be true. I have already commented upon the unreliability of common sense but there is another interesting issue here. The popularity of what an American writer (Hewitt, 1998) has called the "myth of self esteem" probably has a number of sources. One is that it conveniently links what is personally rewarding – feeling good about yourself – with what is socially desirable – a state of mind that reduces social problems. Moreover, singling out lack of self-esteem as the principal alibi for these problems exonerates almost everyone. The politician is excused because the fault lies within the individual and not within social conditions. The culprit is relieved of responsibility because something inside over which he or she had little control is to blame for the misdemeanours. Finally, there is an easy remedy: an esteem-boosting course of treatment. It is unlikely that remedies will be so simple or responsibilities so easily evaded.

- ***But isn't high self-esteem a good thing in itself?*** *"If it makes me feel better, isn't that enough?"*

I think it probably is enough, but like most good things, in moderation. We have perhaps been too concerned to make a case for high self-esteem based on its capacity to deliver other benefits and reduce social problems. It should count in favour of self-esteem that people blessed with enough of it have happier, less troubled lives. So there is a case for investing in efforts to alleviate very low self-esteem for these reasons alone, but most people do not have very low self-esteem (Baumeister, 1998). Further, very high self-esteem is not without its costs when it leads people to despise those who are different from them, to be immune to criticism and advice, and to take foolish risks grounded in entirely unrealistic optimism – all of which are characteristic of this other end of the continuum.

Policies aimed at helping young people make assumptions about the truth of various propositions concerning human nature. These policies are more likely to have their hoped-for effects if these assumptions are well-founded. An almost unprecedented volume of research attention has been directed at self-esteem. In consequence, although our knowledge is by no means perfect or complete, we do now know a great deal about both the determinants of young people's self-esteem and the effects on behaviour of possessing different levels of self-esteem. It is to be hoped, therefore, that future policy, and indeed practice, will make appropriate use of the evidence now available in this area.

References

Abelson, R. P. (1995). *Statistics as principled argument.* Mahwah, NJ: Erlbaum.

Aberson, C., Healy, M., & Romano, V. (2000). Ingroup bias and self-esteem: A meta-analytic review. *Personality and Social Psychology Review*, 4: 157-173.

Armistead, L., Forehand, R., Beach, S., & Brody, G. (1995). Predicting interpersonal competence in young adulthood: The roles of family, self and peer systems during adolescence. *Journal of Child and Family Studies*, 4: 445-460.

Aron, A., Paris, M., & Aron, E. N. (1995). Falling in love: Prospective studies of self-concept change. *Journal of Personality and Social Psychology*, 69: 1102-1112.

Baumeister, R. (1998). The self. In D. T. Gilbert, S. T. Fiske & G. Lindzey (Eds.), *The handbook of social psychology,* Vol. 1. (pp. 680-740). 4th ed. New York: McGraw Hill.

Blaskovich, J., & Tomaka, J. (1991). Measures of self-esteem. In J. P. Robinson, P. R. Shaver & L. S. Wrightsman (Eds.), *Measures of personality and social psychological attitudes* (pp. 115-160). San Diego, CA: Academic Press.

Borhnstedt, G. W., & Felson, R. B. (1983). Explaining the relations among children's actual and perceived performances and self-esteem: A comparison of several causal models. *Journal of Personality and Social Psychology*, 45: 43-56.

Button, E. J., Sonuga-Barke, E., Davies, J., & Thompson, M. (1996). A prospective study of self-esteem in the prediction of eating problems in adolescent schoolgirls: Questionnaire findings. *British Journal of Clinical Psychology*, 35:193-203.

Bynner, J., O'Malley, P. M., & Bachman, J. G. (1981). Self-esteem and delinquency revisited. *Journal of Youth and Adolescence*, 10: 407-444.

California Task Force to Promote Self-esteem and Social Responsibility (1990). *Toward a state of self-esteem*. Sacramento, CA: California State Department of Education.

Coopersmith, S. (1967). *The antecedents of self-esteem.* San Fransisco, CA: W.H. Freeman.

Croker, J., & Major, B. (1989). Social stigma and self-esteem: The self protective properties of stigma. *Psychological Review*, 98: 608-630.

Cvetkovich, G., & Grote, B. (1980). Psychosocial development and the social problem of teenage illegitimacy. In C. Chilman (Ed.), *Adolescent pregnancy and childbearing: Findings from research*. Washington, DC: US Department of Health and Human Services.

DeMan, A., F., Leduc, C., & Labreche-Gauthier, L. (1992). Correlates of suicide ideation in French Canadian adults and adolescents: A comparison. *Journal of Clinical Psychology*, 48: 811-816.

Egan, S. K., & Perry, D. D. (1998). Does low self-regard invite victimisation? *Developmental Psychology*, 34: 299-309.

Emler, N. (2001). *Self-esteem: The costs and causes of low self worth*. York: York Publishing Services.

Emler, N., & Reicher, S. (1995). *Adolescence and delinquency: The collective management of reputation*. Oxford: Blackwell.

Feinstein, L. (2000). *The relative economic importance of academic, psychological and behavioural attributes developed in childhood*. Unpublished paper, Centre for Economic Performance, London School of Economics.

Feiring, C., & Taska, L. S. (1996). Family self-concept. Ideas on its meaning. In B. Braken (Ed.), *Handbook of self-concept* (pp. 317-373). New York: Wiley.

Garnefski, N., Diekstra, R. F., & Heus, P. (1992). A population-based survey of the characteristics of high school students with and without a history of suicidal behaviour. *Acta Psychiatrica Scandinavica*, 86: 189-96.

Garris, L., Stecker, A., & Mcintire, J. R. (1976). The relationship between oral contraceptives and adolescent sexual behaviour. *Journal of Sex Research*, 12: 135-146.

Gray-Little, B., & Hafdahl, A. (2000). Factors influencing racial comparisons of self-esteem: A quantitative review. *Psychological Bulletin*, 126: 26-54.

Haney, P., & Durlak, J. A. (1998). Changing self-esteem in children and adolescents: A meta-analytic review. *Journal of Clinical Child Psychology*, 27: 423-433.

Hansford, B. C., & Hattie, J. A. (1982). The relationship between self and achievement/performance motivation. *Review of Educational Research*, 52: 123-142.

Harrison, B. G. (1989). The importance of being Oprah. *The New York Times Magazine*, 11 June: 28-30.

Harter, S. (1998). The development of self-representations. In W. Damon & N. Eisenberg (Eds.), *Handbook of child psychology, social, emotional and personality development,* Vol. 3. (pp. 553-617). New York: Wiley.

Hawker, D. S., & Boulton, M. J. (2000). Twenty years research on peer victimization and psychosocial maladjustment: A meta-analytic review of cross-sectional studies. *Journal of Child Psychology and Psychiatry and Allied Disciplines*, 41: 441-455.

Herrenkohl, E. C., Herrenkojhl, R. C., Egolf, B. P., & Russo, M. J. (1998). The relationship between early maltreatment and teenage parenthood. *Journal of Adolescence*, 21: 291-303.

Hewitt, J. P. (1998). *The myth of self-esteem: Finding happiness and solving problems in America*. New York: St. Martin's Press.

Hoge, D., Smit, E., & Crist, J. (1995). Reciprocal effects of self-concept and academic achievement in sixth and seventh grade. *Journal of Youth and Adolescence*, 24: 295-414.

Hopkins, R. H., Mauss, A. L., Kearney, K. A., & Weisheit, R. A. (1988). Comprehensive evaluation of model alcohol education curriculum. *Journal of Studies on Alcohol*, 49: 38-50.

Jang, S. J., & Thornberry, T. P. (1998). Self-esteem, delinquent peers and delinquency: A test of the self-enhancement thesis. *American Sociological Review*, 63: 568-598.

Kaplan, H. B. (1980). Deviant behaviour and self-enhancement in adolescence. *Journal of Youth and Adolescence*, 7: 253-277.

Kaplan, H. B., Smith, P. B., & Pokorny, A. D. (1979). Psychosocial antecedents of unwed motherhood among indigent adolescents. *Journal of Youth and Adolescence*, 8: 181-207.

Katz, A. (2000). *Leading lads*. London: Topman.

Kendall-Tackett, K. A., Williams, L. M., & Finkelhor, D. (1993). Impact of sexual abuse on children: A review and synthesis of recent empirical studies. *Psychological Bulletin*, 113: 164-180.

Kenny, D. (1994). *Interpersonal perception: A social relations analysis*. New York: Guilford.

Keinhorst, C. W., de Wilde, E. J., & van den Bout, J. (1990). Characteristics of suicide attempters in a population-based sample of Dutch adolescents. *British Journal of Psychiatry*, 156: 243-248.

Kingsbury, S., Hawton, K., Steinhardt, K., & James, A. (1999). Do adolescents who take overdoses have specific psychological characteristics? A comparative study with psychiatric and community controls. *Journal of the American Academy of Child and Adolescent Psychiatry*, 38: 1125-1131.

Kjelsberg, E., Neegaard, E., & Dahl, A. A. (1994). Suicide in adolescent psychiatric inpatients: Incidence and predictive factors. *Acta Psychiatrica Scandinavica*, 89: 235-241.

Kling, K. C., Hyde, J. S., Sowers, C. J., & Buswell, B. N. (1999). Gender differences in self-esteem: A meta-analysis. *Psychological Bulletin*, 125: 470-500.

Kostanski, M., & Gullone, E. (1998). Adolescent body image dissatisfaction: Relationships with self-esteem, anxiety and depression controlling for body mass. *Journal of Child Psychology and Psychiatry and Allied Disciplines*, 39: 255-262.

Laflin, M. T., Moore-Hirschl, S., Weis, D. L., & Hayes, B. E. (1994). Use of the theory of reasoned action to predict drug and alcohol use. *International Journal of Addictions*, 29: 927-940.

Luker, K. (1975). *Taking chances: Abortion and the decision not to contracept.* Berkeley, CA: University of California Press.

Lyman, D. R., Mikich, R., & Zimmerman, R. (2000). Project DARE: No effects at 10-year follow-up. *Journal of Consulting and Clinical Psychology*, 67: 590-593.

McCarthy, J. D., & Hoge, D. (1984). The dynamics of self-esteem and delinquency. *American Journal of Sociology*, 90: 396-410.

McCauley, G. T. (1995). The relationship of self-esteem and locus of control to unintended pregnancy and childbearing among adolescent females. *Dissertation Abstracts International: Section B, The Sciences and Engineering*. 55, No 7-B, 2678.

MacCorquodale, P., & DeLamater, J. (1978). Self-image and premarital sexuality. *Journal of Marriage and the Family*, 41; 327-339.

McGee, R., & Williams, S. (2000). Does low self-esteem predict health compromising behaviours among adolescents? *Journal of Adolescents*, 23: 569-582.

McNair, L. D., Carter, J. A., & Williams, M. K. (1998). Self-esteem, gender and alcohol use: Relationships with HIV risk perception and behaviors in college students. *Journal of Sex and Marital Therapy*, 24: 29-36.

Marcioan, P. L., & Kazdin, A. E. (1994). Self-esteem, depression, hopelessness and suicidal intent among psychiatrically disturbed inpatient children. *Journal of Clinical Child Psychology*, 23: 151-160.

Neumark-Sztainer, D., Storey, M., French, S.A., & Resnick, M. D. (1997). Psychosocial correlates of health compromising behaviors among adolescents. *Health Education Research*, 12: 37-52.

Olmstead, R. E., Guy, S. M., O'Malley, P. M., & Bentler, P. M. (1991). Longitudinal assessment of the relationship between self-esteem, fatalism, loneliness and substance abuse. *Journal of Social Behavior and Personality*, 6: 749-770.

Petty. J., & Wegener, D. T. (1998). Attitude change: Multiple roles for persuasion variables. In D. T. Gilbert, S. T. Fiske & G. Lindzey (Eds.), *The handbook of social psychology,* Vol. 1. (pp.323-390). New York: McGraw Hill.

Petrie, K., Chamberlain, K., & Clark D. (1988). Psychological predictors of future suicidal behaviour in hospitalized suicide attempters. *British Journal of Clinical Psychology*, 27: 247-257.

Plotnick, R. D., & Butler, S. S. (1991). Attitudes and adolescent non-marital childbearing: Evidence from the National Longitudinal Study of Youth. *Journal of Adolescent Research*, 6: 470-492.

Rabe, J. J. (1998). Body image disturbances in anorexia nervosa. *Psychiatria Polska*, 32 (supplement): 15-23.

Rhodes, N., & Wood, W. (1992). Self-esteem and intelligence affect influenceability: The mediating role of message reception. *Psychological Bulletin*, 111: 156-171.

Robbins, C., Kaplan, H. B., & Martin, S. S. (1985). Antecedents of pregnancy among unmarried adolescents. *Journal of Marriage and the Family*, 42: 567-583.

Rosenberg, M. (1965). *Society and the adolescent self-image*. Princeton, NJ: Princeton University Press.

Rosenberg, M., & Pearlin, L. I. (1978). Social class and self-esteem among children and adults. *American Journal of Sociology*, 84: 53-77.

Ross, H. E., & Ivis, F. (1999). Binge eating and substance abuse among male and female adolescents. *International Journal of Eating Disorders*, 26: 245-260.

Rubin, M., & Hewstone, M. (1998). Social identity theory's self-esteem hypothesis: A review and some suggestions for clarification. *Review of Personality and Social Psychology*, 2: 40-62.

Scheff, T. J., Retzinger, S. M., & Ryan, M. T. (1989). Crime, violence and self-esteem: Review and proposals. In A. M. Mecca, N. J. Smelser & J. Vasconcellos (Eds.), *The social importance of self-esteem* (pp. 165-199). Berkeley, CA: University of California Press.

Scheier, L. M., Botvin, G.J., Griffin, K. W., & Diaz, T. (2000). Dynamic growth models of self-esteem and adolescent alcohol use. *Journal of Early Adolescence*, 20: 178-209.

Shisslak, C. M., Crago, M., & Estes, L. S. (1995). The spectrum of eating disturbances. *International Journal of Eating Disorders*, 18: 209-219.

Silbereisen, R. K., Schoenpflug, U., & Albrecht, H. T. (1990). Smoking and drinking: prospective analyses in German and Polish adolescents. In K. Hurrelmann & F. Loesel (Eds.), *Health hazards in adolescence: Prevention and intervention in childhood and adolescence* (pp. 167-190). Berlin: Walter de Gruyter.

Skager, R., & Kerst, E. (1989). Alcohol and drug use and self-esteem: A psychological perspective. In A. M. Mecca, N. J. Smelser & J. Vasconcellos (Eds.), *The social importance of self-esteem* (pp. 248-293). Berkeley, CA: University of California Press.

Smelser, N. J. (1989). Self-esteem and social problems: An introduction. In A. M. Mecca, N. J. Smelser & J. Vasconcellos (Eds.), *The social importance of self-esteem* (pp. 1-23). Berkeley, CA: University of California Press.

Stanley, L., & Arora, T. (1998). Social exclusion among adolescent girls: Their self-esteem and coping strategies. *Educational Psychology in Practice*, 14: 94-100.

Stoil, M. J., Hill, G. A., Jansen, M. A., Sambranao, S., & Winn, F. J. (2000). Benefits of community based demonstration efforts: Knowledge gained in substance abuse. *Journal of Community Psychology*, 28: 375-389.

Tajfel, H. (1978). *Differentiation between social groups: Studies in the social psychology of inter-group relations*. London: Academic Press.

Taylor, S., & Brown, J. D. (1988). Illusion and well-being: A psychological perspective on mental health. *Psychological Bulletin*, 103: 193-210.

Van Gstel, A., Schotte, C., & Maes, M. (1997). The prediction of suicide intent in depressed patients. *Acta Psychiatrica Scandinavica*, 96: 254-259.

Vela, M. L., Persic, S., & Lester, D. (1996). Does self-esteem predict suicidality after controls for depression? *Psychological Reports*, 79: 1178.

Veron-Guidry, S., Williamson, D. A., & Netemeyer, R. G. (1977). Structural modelling analysis of body dysphoria and eating disorder symptoms in preadolescent girls. *Eating Disorder: The Journal of Treatment and Prevention*, 5: 15-27.

Waller, G. (2001). *The relation between self-esteem and eating disorders*. Paper presented at BPS Developmental and Educational Psychology Conference, Worcester, September 2001.

Wells, E. L., & Rankin, J. H. (1983). Self-concept as a mediating factor in delinquency. *Social Psychology Quarterly*, 46: 11-22.

West, C. K., Fish, J. A., & Stevens, R. J. (1980). General self-concept, self-concept of academic ability and school achievement: Implications for 'causes' of self-concept. *American Journal of Education*, 24: 194-213.

West, P., & Sweeting, H. (1997). 'Lost souls' and 'rebel': A challenge to the assumption that low self-esteem and unhealthy lifestyles are associated. *Health Education*, 5: 161-167.

Willcox, M., & Sattler, D. N. (1996). The relationship between eating disorders and depression. *Journal of Social Psychology*, 136: 269-271.

Williams, G. J., Power, K. G., & Millar, H. R. (1993). Comparison of eating disordered and other dietary/weight groups in measures of perceived control, assertiveness, self-esteem and self directed hostility. *International Journal of Eating Disorders*, 14: 27-31.

Wiltfang, G. L, & Scarbecz, M. (1990). Social class and adolescents' self-esteem: Another look. *Social Psychology Quarterly*, 53: 174-183.

Winefiled, H. R., Winefield, A. H. Tiggermann, M., & Goldney, R. D. (1989). Psychosocial concomitants of tobacco and alcohol use in young Australian adults. *British Journal of Addiction*, 84: 1067-1073.

Wood, A., Waller, G., & Gowers, S. (1994). Predictors of eating psychopathology in adolescent girls. *Eating Disorders Review*, 2: 6-14.

Author Biography

Nicholas Emler is currently Professor of Social Psychology at the University of Surrey. He has previously held professorial appointments at the Universities of Dundee and Oxford, the London School of Economics, and Université Rene Descartes, Paris, and has been a visiting professor at the Johns Hopkins University, the Ecole des Hautes Etudes en Sciences Sociales in Paris, and the Universities of Bologna, Geneva and Tulsa. He has previously published research on moral development in childhood, delinquency, and socio-cognitive development; his present research interests include social development in adolescence, political socialisation, gossip, and leadership. He is currently preparing a report for the Joseph Rowntree Foundation on young people and relationships.

Self-esteem and youth development: a youth work perspective

John Huskins

Introduction

In response to Emler's (2001) research report on the causes and cost of low self-worth I start by confessing to three related prejudices based on over 30 years experience in assessing and promoting youth work nationally, as these may become apparent as I proceed. These are:

- I question some aspects of academic research in the youth field for its tediousness and expense. I usually find informed professional assessment more useful, such as that carried out by the pre-OFSTED HM Inspectorate of Schools Youth Work Team.

- I criticise those psychologists who oversimplify and fail to recognise the complexity of what they are measuring, rather than emphasising the importance of holistic approaches that defy their box ticking and number crunching tendencies.

- I am against those sociologists, who, while they are good at telling you what the problem is, rarely, if ever, give you usable solutions.

I was interested to discover whether these prejudices would be confirmed or confronted by Emler's conclusions and if social psychology would prove a helpful guide to working with disaffected young people. Despite the above prejudices, I did find the research review stimulating and useful as a catalyst in helping to develop my own thinking on the subject. I had not realised that so many claims had been made for self-esteem being the panacea for all ills. It is not surprising that the research evidence challenges this claim. What is being measured often appears to be a very simplistic interpretation of what most youth workers mean when they use the term 'self-esteem' as a helpful shorthand for a group of attitudes, feelings and skills, and associated social skills – a complex mix of skills addressing young people's behaviours holistically.

An overview of Emler's research report

By means of considering the relevance of the research report by Emler I offer a non-academic and youth work perspective overview on the main points of his review.

Aim of the report

The report examines popular beliefs about self-esteem, developed over centuries, correctly claiming perhaps, that they are imprecise and have not necessarily been supported by research evidence. It challenges the assumption by some that self-esteem is the antidote to all social ills. For example, it highlights the belief held by some teachers, mainly in the past, that children must never experience failure as this would damage their self-esteem, and thus competitive sports are out. However, it is easy to caricature popular beliefs in this way and then dismiss them as untenable, without recognising the elements of truth which they may contain. I would maintain that common sense is, nevertheless, a useful test when assessing the results of academic research.

It recognises that in popular usage self-esteem is about psychological health, about motivations, about personal identity. Yet, it rightly goes on to criticise those who have made exaggerated claims for self-esteem and who have used this uncritically to justify investment in unproven programmes, particularly in the United States, where most of this research originates.

Measuring self-esteem

Much of the research on self-esteem seems to assume that an individual's self-esteem is an attitude concerned with their opinion of themselves, possibly based on what an individual believes others think of them rather than an objective quality. The most frequently used measure of self-esteem, the Rosenberg Self-Esteem Scale (Rosenberg, 1965) is based on responses (agree or not) to the following ten self-report statements:

1. On the whole I am satisfied with myself.
2. At times I think I am no good at all.
3. I think that I have a number of good qualities.
4. I am able to do things as well as most other people.
5. I feel I do not have much to be proud of.
6. I certainly feel useless at times.
7. I feel I am a person of worth, at least on an equal plane with others.
8. I wish I could have more respect for myself.
9. All in all, I am inclined to feel that I am a failure.
10. I take a positive attitude towards myself.

The report claims that this test achieves a high level of precision with adolescents. However, I find it hard to believe that the disaffected adolescents found in many youth projects would be able to interpret these statements as intended, let alone provide consistent answers. Further, in any case, what is it measuring? Is this self-esteem as we understand it or an oversimplification to suit the research tool?

Three other self-report measurement tools are mentioned; Coopersmith Self-esteem Inventory (1967), Tennessee Self-concept Scale (Fitts, 1965) and The Piers-Harris Children's Self-concept Scale (Piers, 1967). The Coppersmith Self-esteem Inventory (1967) – an aggregate measure of self-esteem in four different areas of life: parents, peers, school, interests – does not, apparently provide consistent results compared with the Rosenberg Self-esteem Scale but the others do. Observer-based ratings of personality are usually consistent with self-reports, but are not with self-esteem. Thus, doubt is raised about what is being measured by the Rosenberg Self-esteem Scale. Indirect measures were also found not to correlate with the Rosenberg Self-esteem Scale; questioning, again, its validity. Correlations with measures of depression, locus of control, self-efficacy and neuroticism were explored, suggesting some relationship between these characteristics, as might be expected.

The relationship between self-esteem, as measured by the above tests – mainly the Rosenberg Self-esteem Scale – and behaviour is then examined. However, from the descriptions given it seems that programmes designed to improve self-esteem alone are usually being considered (this is not stated, but it is said that it is very important to exclude other influences). If this is so, they are very unlikely to bear much similarity to the majority of youth programmes that address a range of attitudes and social skills, not always specified, in addition to self-esteem. This point is referred to again below.

The report also refers to other factors influencing research outcomes, including direct causes; mediators; indirect causes; moderators; correlated outcomes, and effects. It goes on to say that virtually all the research programmes studied do not differentiate between these various factors and, thus, cannot be used to verify the effect of self-esteem one way or the other. Further, longitudinal studies and true experiments are said to be necessary to validate research results, but neither approach appears to have been followed with self-esteem because of the difficulties involved, again putting their validity in doubt.

Self-esteem and links to behaviour

Criminal behaviour

The correlation between low self-esteem and criminal behaviour is considered. While claims have been made suggesting that offending is an attempt to gain self-esteem in the eyes of the peer group, with the implication that those with high self-esteem are less likely to offend, the research evidence is again unclear. Some evidence suggests that those with high self-esteem are more likely to be involved in violent crime if their view of themselves is challenged. Overall, the research results are inconclusive.

Racial prejudice

With racial prejudice and its links to low self-esteem, the research findings are again inconclusive, with some suggestion that limited education is a factor. Another significant factor, not mentioned, would be empathy, based on personal experience of living and working with those from different racial groups rather than on stereotypes.

Educational attainment

Educational underachievement is a major concern of the present Government and has, apparently, received most research attention. The conclusion given is that there is a relationship between self-esteem and educational attainment, but it is not strong. However, it also states that there are many other factors influencing achievement, including parental support, age, gender, ethnic origin, socio-economic background and the educational outcome considered. Separating these from self-esteem is not easy. This would seem to be the problem of only considering self-esteem in isolation when these and other factors, such as social skills, can have a major effect. The correlation with education-specific self-esteem is stronger. Ability, effort and expectations also vary widely and influence outcomes. Emler (*ibid.*: 28) concludes this section noting that, "one other curious difference is that people with high self-esteem can show higher persistence at a task but in such a way that results in no consistent advantage. This is because the persistence is often counter-productive, it can be wasted effort on lost causes". However, with no evidence to justify this it may be a possibility in some circumstances, but not necessarily be so in general.

Other behaviours

Though different factors apply, abuse of illegal drugs and smoking has been attributed to low self-esteem.The research evidence is inconclusive, mainly because other factors cannot be discounted. There is little evidence to link smoking with self-esteem, but with alcohol abuse a relation with depression which is related to self-esteem is evident. In relation to risky sexual behaviour, an association with self-esteem is accepted, though the complexity of the behaviour makes achieving clear-cut research findings difficult. With health risks, there is evidence that medium self-esteem is an indicator. It is suggested that this is possibly because those with high self-esteem resist harmful influences, while those with low self-esteem do not notice the risk. With child mal-treatment, the research evidence is inconclusive. Chronic dependence on state support is another area where the evidence is inconclusive. With eating disorders, there is, again, no conclusive evidence. It is difficult to carry out research into suicide, parasuicide and suicidal thoughts and the evidence available is once more inconclusive. Yet, in the conclusions it is stated that those with low self-esteem are more likely to "have suicidal thoughts and make suicide attempts" (Emler, 2001: 59).

It is recognised that self-esteem interacts with other risk factors, but in unknown ways. The criticisms that the measures of self-esteem based on self-report are inaccurate and measure the wrong things are recognised as possible or likely, thus questioning the validity of most, if not all, the research findings considered.

Differences in self-esteem

Sources of differences in self-esteem are considered and summarised as:

- ***Weak or no effect:*** race or ethnicity; social class; gender.
- ***Modest effect:*** successes and failures; rejections and acceptances; appearance.
- ***Substantial effect:*** parent behaviour, genes.

There is no clear evidence that significant others influence self-esteem as strongly as parents, but this is complicated by the influence and complexity of relationships. Social exclusion, which may result from unemployment, might also be expected to lead to low self-esteem, but evidence is lacking. From a youth work perspective, one would expect the factors listed as having 'modest effect' as well as 'substantial' effect, thus, questioning the validity of this research.

Conclusions of Emler's research report

While the report suggests that programmes vary widely in terms of successfully raising self-esteem, it concludes that overall there is very little evidence that any interventions work. However, some programmes also aim to develop social skills, and are similar to youth programmes, but the general conclusions given do not differentiate between these two types of approach. It is admitted that current evidence prevents decisions on why effective programmes work. However, one successful programme in raising self-esteem is cited (Mruk, 1999), listing a range of interventions that align with effective youth work programmes. For example:

- Developing problem-solving.
- Being accepted and caring.
- Providing consistent affirming feedback (emphasising the positive).
- Cognitive restructuring (essentially changing attitudes and perceptions).
- Assertiveness training (empowerment).
- Modelling (for example, demonstrating a more effective way of handling conflict).
- Using 'natural self-esteem moments', magnifying positive effects of major transitions.

In summary of Emler's report, most of the assessments of the nature of research and the evidence on the relationship between self-esteem and behaviour emphasise the deficiencies of most of this research, including:

- Lack of agreement of what is meant by self-esteem.
- The three main tests for self-esteem measure different things, and are not consistent.
- What is measured is a very simplistic version of a complex characteristic (attitude or feeling?).
- Other factors (unspecified) also influence and are influenced by 'self-esteem' (as measured).
- The samples of young people used were unreliable and influenced the results.
- Control groups and longitudinal studies were very rare, but are necessary for reliable results.
- Any link between 'self-esteem' and behaviour is complex, and most research is inconclusive.
- 'Self-esteem' may be consequence rather than cause or that 'self-esteem' and the behaviour of interest are both influenced by something else, but to an unknown extent.
- As concluded by Emler (*ibid.*: 58), "much research has not been up to the task of analysing these links adequately and is therefore virtually useless in answering the critical question: does 'self-esteem' affect behaviour or not?"

The following conclusions are supported, albeit with varying degrees of certainty, by research.

Young people with very low self-esteem are more likely to:

- show symptoms of depression; be more often unhappy.
- become pregnant as teenagers (girls).
- have suicidal thoughts and make suicide attempts.
- experience in their twenties longer periods of unemployment and earn less (males).
- suffer from eating disorders (if they are female).
- be victimised.
- fail to respond to social influence.
- have more difficulty forming and sustaining successful close relationships.

Young people with low self-esteem are not more likely as a result to:

- commit crimes, including violent crimes.
- use or abuse illegal drugs.
- drink alcohol to excess or smoke.
- as parents, physically or sexually abuse their own children.
- fail academically.

These conclusions are very misleading if taken at face value. In the context of the research deficiencies and weaknesses listed they surely cannot be supported and are potentially harmful.

It is interesting that when reviewing the results of the Californian Task Force Project (1990) it was reported that the data had been interpreted selectively to give the results they wanted. One would hope that this has not been the case here, that is to make the results of the project appear more conclusive than they really are, rather than inconclusive, which would seem to be the only valid conclusion to make. In any case, whatever the results, they are of limited relevance in practice because the vast majority of projects addressing youth at risk behaviours do not focus on raising self-esteem as the only or main objective. Self-esteem is one of many factors being addressed, and even then 'self-esteem' is used to mean something much more complex than which is being measured by the standard tests.

One conclusion in the report is particularly revealing. Referring to the risk of teenage pregnancy, Emler (2001: 61) states that "low self-esteem appears to be a risk factor but improving the knowledge and skills required to use contraception effectively may nonetheless be a more cost-effective way of reducing the risk". However, other recent research has demonstrated that the majority of pregnant teenage girls in the research group had engaged in comprehensive sex and contraceptive education, but that this alone is not effective. Not surprisingly, having unprotected sex isn't a rational decision. Other emotional and social factors are at play. Many working in the youth field would recognise that social skills are needed, including assertiveness training, in addition to self-esteem, using this in a broad sense.

Self-esteem and youth programmes for disaffected young people

Based on long experience of assessing and promoting youth work practice with disaffected young people, I have to admit that there is much poor practice, with imprecise objectives, ill-defined methods of intervention and little accountability in terms of learning outcomes and behavioural change. I argue that most risk behaviours (i.e., school underachievement, truancy and exclusion; drugs misuse; risky sexual behaviour leading to unintended pregnancies and STDs/Aids; emotional problems leading to suicide attempts; and crime) can only be addressed successfully by a combination of education and the development of social skills, including self-esteem (*see* Huskins, 1996). In other words, a holistic approach is needed to address risk behaviours as interconnected and requiring an integrated social skills approach, in addition to factual education and information. Single-issue projects are unlikely to be successful as most 'at risk' young people will be involved in a number of these behaviours, not just one. Unfortunately, for academic researchers, young people's behaviour is complex and does not respond to simplistic analysis.

Consider, for example, school underachievement, truancy and exclusion, with young people at Key Stages 3 and 4, which is being addressed by the Department for Education and Skills (DfES) 'Excellence in Cities' (EiC) and Connexions programmes. My own experience tells me that if disaffected students are going to be helped to benefit from and contribute to normal classroom learning, without disrupting the learning of others, they need to develop a combination of moderate self-esteem and priority social skills. That is, a package of skills is needed which have to be addressed together (*see* Table One).

Table One

Developmental needs of working with disaffected young people

Developing self-esteem in a youth work context involves a complex mixture of attitudes:

- Improved self concept (e.g., necessary to give experience of success, counter past failure and resist peer group pressure) and an accurate self-image based on self-awareness and appropriate role models, together with.
- A positive life-view, something to look forward to and work for, linked to motivation (e.g., hope, rather than resignation such as "there are no jobs anyway so why bother").
- A commitment to control or change their lives (e.g., recognising that only they can do this, not being dependent on others, accepting that they themselves by their own effort can achieve a worthwhile future).

Developing priority social skills:

- Improved self-esteem, as described above.
- Recognising and managing feelings (e.g., impulse and stress control, defer gratification, develop alternative strategies to violence for addressing conflict).
- Understand and identify with others (empathy) (e.g., to recognise the feelings, needs and points of view of other pupils and teachers, or victims of crime).
- Values development (to identify, understand and explore alternatives to current values, beliefs and behaviour, and their consequences, particularly in relation to the school ethos).

I recognise that a purist may find this complex mixture of attributes unacceptable, and that these attributes could defy research assessment, but that does not necessarily mean they are not valid and useful.

This is why I find much of the research evidence on self-esteem simplistic and clinical. It can be unrelated to the challenges facing youth workers, learning mentors (in DfES 'Excellence in Cities' Initiatives), or personal advisers (in Connexions) when they are working with disaffected young people in trying to improve their academic achievement, reduce truancy and exclusions, and address other risk behaviours. Self-esteem is one element in the equation, and its significance alongside the other three priority skills will vary with the particular risk behaviour and with each individual's circumstances. A complex learning mix is needed, including self-esteem, managing feelings, empathy with others, and values development. It would, in fact, be virtually impossible to attempt to raise self-esteem without promoting these social skills.

The complexity of working with disaffected young people is increased when other wider social skills are added to the priority social skills that are noted above (*see* Table Two). The development of these skills is necessary in order to help each young person to address or avoid risk behaviours, cope with the challenges of adolescence and to negotiate the transitions to adult responsibilities, including training and work.

Table Two

Wider social skills for addressing disaffection in young people

Wider social skills:

- Communication skills, including assertiveness skills.
- Interpersonal and relationship skills.
- Problem-solving (including decision-making, particularly in terms of interpersonal issues, the ability to set attainable goals, linked to self-control and delaying gratification).
- Negotiation.
- Planning and reviewing skills (linked to study skills).

Skilled youth workers help young people to identify their learning needs from this checklist of social skills and then apply a repertoire of one-to-one responses, games, group work and drama activities to encourage their development (*see* Huskins, 1996; 2000). They also recognise the need to address the lower sections of Maslow's (1968) hierarchy of needs (e.g., physiological, safety and belonging) before starting on self-esteem as the basis for cognitive, aesthetic and self-actualisation, the main purpose of the National Curriculum in schools.

The curriculum development model: a holistic approach to developing self-esteem through learning

The same youth work principles can be applied to schools (*see* Huskins, 2001). While self-esteem, as described above, is an important element in addressing disaffection, in particular in encouraging young people to take control of their lives, no claims are made about its importance to individuals in isolation. Self-esteem is seen as a variable element along-side other important elements. The Curriculum Development Model (CDM) (*see* Diagram One) is a model that has proved to be valuable for youth workers and teachers in explaining how these priority and other social skills can be developed and students encouraged to progressively take increasing responsibility for their activities, their learning, themselves and each other.

Stage 1 in the Curriculum Development Model will consist of an initial meeting with a young person to begin assessing his or her priority needs. It is very likely that the priority social skills listed above are weak (e.g., self-esteem, managing feelings, empathy with other students and teachers, and values in relation to the school ethos). A programme will be devised, continuing with one-to-one work at Stage 2, negotiating a programme based on interests, leading into group work at Stage 3. During Stage 3 young people socialise with other students, work on the priority social skills and plan activities to undertake together at Stage 4. As in Connexions, this could be led by a Learning Mentor or Personal Adviser, but more usually will involve others, such as youth workers. These activities encourage team-building and social skills, especially if the Youth Achievement Awards (Bronze) are used to recognise and accredit their achievements. Stage 5, 'sharing responsibility', is the stage that students must reach if they are to benefit from classroom learning, share responsibility for their learning with teachers, careers education and from work experience, and gain and retain employment. Whilst the

Diagram One: Empowering young people – progressive levels of responsibility (Curriculum Development Model)

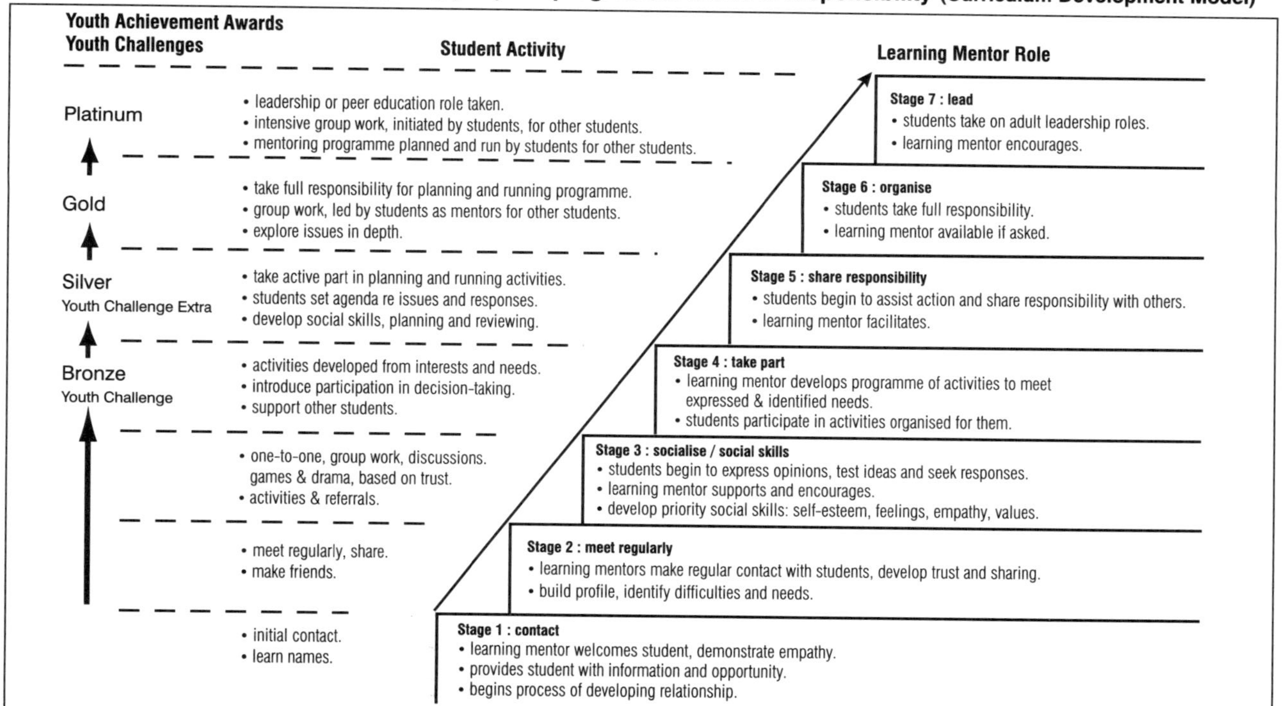

Youth Achievement Awards
Youth Challenges
Student Activity
Learning Mentor Role
Platinum
• leadership or peer education role taken.
• intensive group work, initiated by students, for other students.
• mentoring programme planned and run by students for other students.
Gold
• take full responsibility for planning and running programme.
• group work, led by students as mentors for other students.
• explore issues in depth.
Silver
Youth Challenge Extra
• take active part in planning and running activities.
• students set agenda re issues and responses.
• develop social skills, planning and reviewing.
Bronze
Youth Challenge
• activities developed from interests and needs.
• introduce participation in decision-taking.
• support other students.
• one-to-one, group work, discussions. games & drama, based on trust.
• activities & referrals.
• meet regularly, share.
• make friends.
• initial contact.
• learn names.
Stage 7 : lead
• students take on adult leadership roles.
• learning mentor encourages.
Stage 6 : organise
• students take full responsibility.
• learning mentor available if asked.
Stage 5 : share responsibility
• students begin to assist action and share responsibility with others.
• learning mentor facilitates.
Stage 4 : take part
• learning mentor develops programme of activities to meet expressed & identified needs.
• students participate in activities organised for them.
Stage 3 : socialise / social skills
• students begin to express opinions, test ideas and seek responses.
• learning mentor supports and encourages.
• develop priority social skills: self-esteem, feelings, empathy, values.
Stage 2 : meet regularly
• learning mentors make regular contact with students, develop trust and sharing.
• build profile, identify difficulties and needs.
Stage 1 : contact
• learning mentor welcomes student, demonstrate empathy.
• provides student with information and opportunity.
• begins process of developing relationship.

A progressive model of learning mentor involvement with students (after Gloucestershire Youth and Community Service).

© John Huskins.

completion of these Awards will raise self-esteem (by recognising achievements) their main purpose is much wider in terms of motivating students and developing their social and study skills.

Stages 1–4 represent the initial 'induction phase' before students return full-time to the classroom at Stage 5, still supported informally by the Learning Mentor or Personal Adviser as necessary, hence the 'partnership phase'. This approach is intended for Key Stage 4 (Years 10 and 11) but a similar programme can be used at Key Stage 3 (Years 7, 8 and 9) using the Youth Challenges to recognise and accredit students' achievements (*see* Huskins, 2001). Keeping to the school example, those students targeted by Learning Mentors and Connexions Personal Advisers will be underachieving and frequently displaying what is euphemistically called 'challenging behaviour'. Learning Mentors and Personal Advisers will agree their respective target groups, with the latter tending to take the more demanding students, especially in Year 11.

The Youth Achievement Awards recognise and accredit students' achievements, and encourage social and study skills through the peer education approach of the students agreeing and assessing each other's 'Challenges'. The Award also encourages the development of study skills as the recording procedures encourage planning, reviewing and simple portfolio building. In schools the Awards are operated by the Award Scheme Development and Accreditation Network (ASDAN), and in youth work they are operated by UK Youth and accredited by ASDAN to national standards. The Awards are used throughout the country through the youth service and have only recently been introduced into schools. They have proved extremely successful in re-motivating disaffected young people and raising self-esteem.

The Gold and Platinum Awards are unlikely to be used with these students, but other students in the school can organise activities, for example, through the school council or anti-bullying peer mentoring, and use these as Gold Award Challenges. As confidence is gained with the Bronze Youth Achievement Award, the Silver Award can be used to introduce Key Skills in 'communication', 'working with others' and 'improving own learning and performance'. With guidance, evidence required for assessment is also accumulated 'painlessly' by the young people in the course of completing the Challenges, thus preparing students for employability. Similar approaches apply to Key Stage 3, using the Youth Challenges (a junior version of the Youth Achievement Awards) to accredit participation (CDM Stage 4) or peer mentoring (CDM Stage 5). The examples above are taken from work with schools (Huskins, 2001). For those working with young people outside schools, particularly in Connexions, see Huskins (2001).

Conclusion

This summary of how youth workers address risk behaviours based on a social skills approach, including raising self-esteem, puts self-esteem (as previously defined, *see* Table One, p.36) in perspective as one variable element in a spectrum of needs being addressed holistically. This fits in with the evidence in the research review, that the definition of self-esteem used for research measurements is over simplified, that the results when applied to individual risk behaviours are variable, and that other factors frequently have a determining effect on the results. It would be of interest to examine the extent to which social skills are one of the 'other factors'. The review could have considered more fully the interaction between self-esteem and social skills, as developing social skills, alongside raising self-esteem, is an important part of working with disaffected young people. Another strong conclusion to come out of the research is that parents have a very significant impact on the growing child and his or her self-esteem, but this is hardly a surprise.

Overall, based on the evidence available in the report, I would maintain that the academic research reviewed here into the causes and effects of self-esteem is of questionable quality and demonstrates little, if any, relevance to the real world of working with disaffected young people. So in part, some of my prejudices against academic research in the youth field, psychologists and sociologists seem to have been reinforced by this exercise. They are further strengthened by the most frequently found conclusion of this study of research reported by Emler, that more research is needed. Good research, yes (only qualified in this way at the end), but this review reads like an indictment of the quality of research in this field. The first priority should be to establish credibility, rather than to encourage further flawed research into self-esteem. In the meantime, it might be wiser to trust the judgement of many experienced educators who are competent to assess and manage complex educational issues, and not to ignore common sense.

References

California Task Force to Promote Self-Esteem and Personal and Social Responsibility. (1990). *Toward a state of self-esteem*. Sacramento, CA: California State Department of Education.

Coopersmith, S. (1967). *The antecedents of self-esteem*. San Francisco, CA: W.H. Freeman.

Huskins, J. (1996). *Quality work with young people*. Bristol: John Huskins.

Huskins, J. (2000). *From disaffection to social inclusion*. Bristol: John Huskins.

Huskins, J. (2001). *Priority steps to inclusion: Addressing underachievement, truancy and exclusion at Key Stages 3 & 4*. Bristol: John Huskins.

Maslow, A. (1968). *Towards a psychology of learning*. New York: Wiley.

Mruk, C. (1999). *Self-esteem: Research, theory and practice*. London: Free Association Books.

Rosenberg, M. (1965). *Society and the adolescent self-image*. Princeton, NJ: Princeton University Press.

Author Biography

John Huskins was an HM Inspector of Schools and youth work specialist for 18 years. He is now an Education Consultant assessing and providing management support and training for youth and school programmes designed to address disaffection and risk behaviours. His training handbooks, '*Quality work with young people*' and '*From disaffection to social inclusion*' provide proven approaches to address youth disaffection. They incorporate the Youth Achievement Awards (which he created) that provide a peer education approach to recognising and accrediting young people's achievements. His latest handbook, '*Priority Steps to Inclusion – addressing underachievement, truancy and exclusion at Key Stages 3 & 4*' applies the same principles to work in schools with challenging students. He is currently developing training programmes for learning mentors and inclusion teachers, incorporating the Youth Challenges for Key Stage 3 and the Youth Achievement Awards for Key Stage 4. These publications are available from johnhuskins@netgates.co.uk (details on website www.johnhuskins.com).

Barrow Community Learning Partnership: strategies that support the development of self-esteem in young people

Frances Walker & Mason Minnitt

Introduction

The Barrow Community Learning Partnership (BCLP) is an Education Action Zone funded by the Department for Education and Skills (DfES) that works with self-selected schools within Barrow-in-Furness, with an ultimate aim of raising aspirations and achievement within the Zone. Through the Barrow Community Learning Partnership, groups of schools work in partnership with the private sector and with local organisations to develop new approaches to raising standards of education within an area of deprivation.

The levels of social and economic deprivation in six of Barrow's wards are high. In 2000 the local urban area was rated 24th nationally on the deprivation indices. Indications include high levels of long-term unemployment as a result of ill-health, male suicide, teenage pregnancy and drug related crimes. Educationally, Barrow has low retention rates within 16-19 years education, especially in relation to young women, and overall low recruitment into continuing education for post-18 years.

Colleagues in the Barrow Community Learning Partnership share an interest in both research and practice in the area of self-esteem, especially within the context of raising achievement in an Education Action Zone. The following paper is a response to the seminar held by Brathay Hall Trust in which the theme of self-esteem within the context of youth development work was initially discussed from two differing perspectives.

John Huskins – speaking from a youth development perspective – challenged conclusions drawn by Nicholas Emler's research review on self-esteem (Emler, 2001). As part of his challenge Huskins (*see* this volume) provides a holistic model. He focuses on a framework that develops moderate self-esteem in which an individual combines a positive life view with a commitment to take control of and change his or her own life. Huskins also argued that a defining priority necessary to help a young person to address or avoid risk behaviours and make the transition from adolescence to adulthood included social, interpersonal and intrapersonal skills. These skills, Huskins (2002) asserts, are:

- recognising and managing feelings.
- understanding and identifying with others.
- values development.
- communication.
- interpersonal and relationship.
- problem-solving.
- negotiation.
- planning and reviewing.

Emler reminded the audience that the debate about the meaning and content of self-esteem is long-running. He quoted from William James who in 1890 stated that "self-esteem is success divided by pretensions" – i.e. that which a person has achieved measured against his or her aspirations. The central themes of Emler's (2001) paper on self-esteem are that:

- There is not agreement among researchers about the nature of self-esteem. It is either a general feeling about self or a view based on judgements about one's capabilities, value, worth, (self-image and self-efficacy).
- Self-esteem can be measured. Evidence suggests that low self-esteem is rare. Most research focuses on contrasting very high self-esteem with moderate self-esteem.
- Some of the conventional 'wisdom' about the social effects of low self-esteem is not substantiated by evidence, e.g. that it leads to criminal behaviour.
- Parental influence on self-esteem is the most significant factor.
- Planned interventions can raise self-esteem, but there is little knowledge of why or for how long the effect is sustained.

He posed the following three questions:

1. What are the consequences of low self-esteem?
2. What factors and conditions determine a person's level of self-esteem?
3. Can self-esteem be raised through planned interventions?

The debate moved from a critique of research findings to examples of practice based on raising self-esteem, and prompted us to reflect on our own thinking and practice in this area. In light of such reflections we chose to focus our attention on Emler's third question, "Can self-esteem be raised through planned interventions?"

Can self-esteem be raised through planned interventions?

Whilst accepting that measuring changes in self-esteem may pose problems for researchers, there are skills, qualities and dispositions, loosely defined as the components of self-esteem, which are worth enhancing. We concur with Emler's assertion that a view of self-esteem as a 'vaccine' to be administered indiscriminately, falls short of appropriate interventions to support young people's social and emotional development. For this reason, the raising of self-esteem is considered to be a single element within a range of linked strategies used by the Barrow Community Learning Partnership within formal and informal educational settings.

BarroWise: developing interventions for young people

Within the Barrow Community Learning Partnership the focus is not primarily on trying to measure young people's levels of self-esteem and subsequent changes. The focus is on delivering interventions focused on improving thinking skills, teaching and learning strategies and emotional and social skills within a framework – 'BarroWise' – designed to link existing work and targeting the enhancement of emotional resilience and self-esteem, among its intended outcomes. 'BarroWise' takes the work of US psychologist Robert Sternberg (2000); the balance theory of wisdom which is arrived at by considering the needs of oneself balanced against the needs of the community. These ideas are used as a starting point that enables a collection of 'wise' skills and abilities that underpin emotional resilience, resourcefulness and wise thinking, learning and behaviour to be identified. The key themes of the BarroWise framework include:

- thinking and reflection.
- working, living and playing together.
- feeling good about ourselves.
- making wise choices.

A fundamental element of the BarroWise approach is to address how teaching and learning frameworks can incorporate the elements to create Wise Learning Communities that encourage the development of wise students. Wise students will demonstrate, as Claxton (1999: 6) suggests, "the three Rs of learning power: resilience, resourcefulness and reflectiveness." 'Feeling good about ourselves' is a key theme in this work and incorporates self-esteem alongside emotional management, independence and motivation. Practical applications of this framework have included an infant school (staff and children) considering what a wise playground looks, sounds and feels like and identifying what resources and activities would support the development of wise skills. Barrow Community Learning Partnership Zone primary schools have also worked on identifying wise skills and planned the development of such skills throughout areas of the curriculum. The theme of creating learning environments that take account of the affective and social domains, alongside the cognitive demands of academic curricula, are an essential feature of developing 'wise learning communities'. Weare (2000: 5) identifies the common ground that exists between academic learning and social and affective education.

> It is vital that those who seek to promote high academic standards and those who seek to promote mental, emotional and social health realise that they are on the same side, and that social and affective education can support academic learning, not simply take away time from it.

This is a view that the Barrow Community Learning Partnership actively supports and promotes within zone schools.

Identifying the gifts and talents of all young people

The 'Gifted and Talented' policy developed within the Barrow Community Learning Partnership is based on the concept of an inclusive model, promoting a child or young person's gifts and talents in relation to that person's individual learning profile, rather than in relation to the gifts and talents of their peers (*see* Hymer & Michel, 2002). Attention to developing a child or young person's social and emotional skills is explicitly encouraged within any activity designed to enhance a child's particular gifts or talents.

Initiatives, such as Brathay's experiential education programmes, develop skills that incorporate self-esteem in conjunction with elements that help a young person develop and build emotional resilience. It is a person's emotional resilience that will enable progression towards Maslow's highest tier of 'self actualisation', as referred to by Huskins (*see* this volume). It is widely recognised that before a person can develop his or her intellectual capability, emotional and social needs must be satisfactorily met. As Weare (2000: 63) notes, "a sense of positive self-esteem is generally seen as the essential for mental, emotional and social health".

The creation of an Emotional Health Development Co-ordinator post within the Barrow Community Learning Partnership also recognises the importance of the need for a focus on how the emotional aspects of a child's education directly relates to future academic attainment. As part of this professional remit the Co-ordinator is to develop a key liaison role in relation to the developments initiated as part of the Children's Fund in Cumbria. It is anticipated that Barrow Community Learning Partnership projects to support children's emotional health will be congruent with Children's Fund priorities. This is because Barrow Community Learning Partnership sees work undertaken in Zone schools, and beyond, as complementing future Children's Fund activities to enhance the educational experience of children and young people in Barrow.

Ongoing developmental projects for young people

Individual initiatives and projects taking place within schools contribute to building children's self-esteem, their efficacy and to developing their ability to solve problems – the 'building blocks' for creating emotional resilience, as defined by Rutter (1985). Examples of this can be found in projects and initiatives within the Barrow Community Learning Partnership such as:

- ***Consultative Forum:*** children and young people have the opportunity to display and perform their work to representatives from partner organisations, their teachers and invited guests.

- ***School Council Development Project:*** development of ways of working which allow students to make a positive and valued contribution to life and work in their schools and to have an explicit shared ownership of issues which impact on their aspirations, emotional resilience and sense of self-worth. These projects are allied to a zone-wide Student Forum and to further development of the Barrow Children and Young People's Forum.

- ***Philosophy for Children:*** development of 'Communities of Enquiry' that allow higher order thinking skills to be nurtured within a mutually respectful and supportive environment – and encourage exploration of practical issues such as how best can young people be provided with opportunities to be listened to?

- ***The Critical Skills Programme:*** a collaborative learning methodology that strongly emphasises the social, affective and cognitive components of effective learning. "Providing challenge with support: optimising levels of stress: raising self-esteem: engaging positive emotions and attention" (Weatherley, 2000).

- ***Alive and Kicking Arts Festival:*** a festival staged at a professional venue in Barrow town centre, incorporating performance and displays of children and young people's work.

- ***SERIS (Supporting Emotional Resilience in Schools):*** a project funded by Children's Fund which provides dedicated teaching assistant hours to support children and young people, in schools, who are emotionally vulnerable or in distress.

- ***Out-of-Hours Learning:*** targeting disaffected and vulnerable students, with an emphasis on encouraging voluntary attendance, a supportive learning climate, alternative learning styles and greater confidence and autonomy as learners.

- ***The Excellence Challenge Programme:*** a range of activities that focus on boosting the aspirations of young people with no family history of involvement with Further Education or Higher Education. Students have opportunities to work with, for example, health professionals, Wordsworth Trust poets-in-residence, engineers and university lecturers.

- ***Gifted and Talented Summer School:*** where young people across all academic abilities work together on projects designed to extend their normal educational experience.

- ***Year 11 Brathay project at Alfred Barrow School (a DfES designated School in Challenging Circumstances):*** a combination of residential experiential learning weekends supported by weekly after-school study clubs – designed to boost motivation, aspirations, and perseverance in a target group of 40 higher-achieving students.

- ***Solid Ground:*** a Brathay project bringing elements of experiential learning into the school context.

- ***The National Mentoring Programme:*** mentor support provided for secondary students by trained local undergraduate volunteers.

- ***Age Concern/BCLP Building Bridges Project:*** a range of intergenerational projects, the latest involving volunteer older people working with a photographer and poet-in-residence to explore positive memories and aspirations.

- ***NSPCC/BCLP Family Link Worker:*** initially in four schools focusing on projects to boost home-school links and to support the development of an emotionally resilient learning culture.

Whilst the examples given above vary in the extent to which the predominant emphasis is on the intention to raise self-esteem – that emphasis is always an integral part of programmes designed to support the development of a wiser learning culture.

Conclusions

Initiatives at Barrow Community Learning Partnership are not designed to be 'vaccines for self-esteem', as previously referred to by Emler (2001), or 'bolt-on' initiatives to ameliorate problems. They are to be viewed as an intrinsic part of enhancing the delivery of education in Barrow zone schools. They are also viewed as strategies to enhance and enrich the quality of education and the range of skills it supports, develops and promotes. The enhancement of children and young people's self-esteem is, therefore, a forever evolving and encompassing part of an ethos developing within the Barrow Community Learning Partnership as it strives to fulfil its vision of raising achievement and attainment in its partner schools.

Finally, readers who may still wonder whether self-esteem exists as a focus for enhancement within learning might be interested to note the following words by Professor David Hopkins, Director of the Standards and Effectiveness Unit at the Department for Education and Skills, as part of an Education Action Zone Annual Report (DfES, 2001):

> I would like to take this opportunity to remind everyone that it is through high expectations for all, diversity of provision, collaborative working and extending opportunities that we will succeed in providing every pupil with an education that teaches the joy of learning and gives them the skills, confidence and self-esteem to meet the demands of a fast-changing world.

References

Claxton, G. (1999). *Wise up: Learning to live the learning life*. Stafford: Network Education Press.

DfES. (2001). *Education Action Zones – Annual Report 2001*. London: DfES.

Emler, N. (2001). *Self-esteem. The costs and causes of low self-worth*. York: Joseph Rowntree Foundation / YPS.

Huskins, J. (2002). *Self-esteem and youth development*. Paper presented at Self-esteem and Youth Development Seminar, 29 April, Brathay Hall Trust. London.

Hymer, D., & Michel, D. (2002). *Gifted and talented Learners: Creating a policy for inclusion*. London: David Fulton Publishers.

Rutter, M. (1985). Resilience in the face of adversity. Protective factors and resistance to psychiatric disorder. *British Journal of Psychiatry*, 147: 598-6111.

Sternberg, R. J. (2000). Wisdom as a form of giftedness. *Gifted Child Quarterly*, 44: 252-60.

Weare, K. (2000). *Promoting mental social and emotional health: A whole school approach*. London: Routledge.

Weatherley, C. (2000). *Leading the learning school: raising standards of achievement by improving the quality of teaching and learning*. Stafford: Network Educational Press Ltd.

Authors' Biographies

Frances Walker is Emotional Health Development Co-ordinator of Barrow Community Learning Partnership. Fran has worked in a residential special school for children with neurological disabilities and was assistant officer in charge of a children's community home in Lancashire. She worked for Cumbria LEA as an Education Welfare Officer for over 10 years, including a period of secondment where she was responsible for improving links between the providers of Mental Health Services for children and young people and the Education Authority.

Mason Minnitt is Director of Barrow Community Learning Partnership. He has taught in primary and secondary schools, been a part-time lecturer in Further Education, and was a visiting Lecturer for Leicester University on teacher education programmes. Following senior management posts in Leicestershire and Cambridgeshire community colleges, Mason took over as Headteacher of Settlebeck High School, Cumbria in January 1994. Since January 2000 he has been Director (initially in an acting capacity) of Barrow Community Learning Partnership, an Education Action Zone in South Cumbria.

Self-esteem and youth development: the case for a Person-Centred approach

Jennifer C. F. Peel

Introduction

Nicholas Emler's (2001) work on the costs and causes of low self-esteem presents a serious challenge to those of us who are involved in working with young people. His conclusion that self-esteem is unlikely to be affected by therapeutic interventions and is of little consequence in predicting undesirable behaviour raises several questions:

1. Is the raising of self-esteem an outcome of education or therapy that we should strive for?
2. Can we design programmes that will achieve this?
3. Does poor self-esteem lead to undesirable behaviour?
4. Can people have too high self-esteem with consequent undesirable consequences?

A review of our basic understandings regarding how personal development can 'go wrong' may help us address or even discard some of these questions. One particular understanding of human development, the Person-Centred approach, is valuable here not only because it underpins the work of a high proportion of teachers, youth workers, counsellors, and psychotherapists in this country, but also because it presents a radical and illuminating perspective on the self-esteem debate. An understanding of this approach will help to highlight the flaws in Emler's challenge to current youth work by showing that his positivist approach is too simplistic to have anything of value to contribute to the practical issue of how we should work with young people.

A Person-Centred approach to personal development

Person-Centred theory holds that people are born with two competing motivational systems at work in their self-structure (Rogers, 1951; Thorne, 1992). One motivation is to grow and develop towards achieving one's full potential. In the service of this 'Actualising Tendency' an internal valuing process operates to enable people to place values on experience. By tapping into this internal, deep level of knowing, they decide for themselves what is good, harmless or decidedly bad for them. The Actualising Tendency works to ensure that people will naturally choose to align themselves with behaviours, experiences, values and people who will facilitate their growth. Where growth is not possible (because circumstances do not facilitate it) the Actualising Tendency will ensure that, at the minimum, a person will maintain himself or herself by shunning those things that are harmful. Provided that nothing interferes with this motivational tendency (and with the guiding wisdom of the internal valuing process), a baby or a child can and will develop towards his or her full potential (or, if he or she is unable to do so will at least protect himself or herself from harm).

If we relate this theory to the development of self-esteem, we see that it tells us that people are innately predisposed to be appreciative, valuing and accepting of themselves – because that is a prerequisite for constructive personal development. Whenever this self-appreciation is in place we, therefore, see people behaving in ways that are self-respecting, self-supportive and growth promoting.

How then do most of us end up limited and with dysfunctional, self-injurious and self-doubting aspects of our personalities and behaviours? The answer to this question lies in the presence of a parallel motivational tendency that tends to switch off the Actualising Tendency. This second motivation is the drive to seek love, acceptance and approval from the people around us. Without this support people in general, and the young in particular, cannot thrive. However, the need for approval becomes like a fly in the ointment because those around us, instead of giving us unconditional love, give us love that is conditional on our doing things of which they approve. From this we learn that we cannot earn love for who we intrinsically and authentically are, or for following the path to self-development that is growthful for us. Instead, we learn that we are only loved, approved of and supported when we do, think and value what others think we should. In this way the conditional nature of the love we are given turns us away from the path towards growth that is individually right for us and instead leads us to adopt one that is determined by the 'shoulds' and 'oughts' imposed on us by others. Consequently, the second motivational tendency clashes with and distorts the Actualising Tendency. So instead of choosing what is positive and growthful, people end up choosing those things that will earn them approval by others, even when they comprise damaging choices for the self. A young man who, in spite of his fear, chooses to gain 'street credibility' by joining his friends in a high speed chase in a stolen car would be an example of this sort of choice.

In the context of self-esteem, this clash of motivational tendencies causes people to lose faith in themselves and to value themselves only when they are being what others want them to be. Through this process a fundamental level of confusion and self-doubt is acquired, for at the point where the voice of the Actualising Tendency is drowned out by the person's search for conditional acceptance, distortions develop within the person's ability to evaluate experience. This may lead a person towards either self-hatred, or self-aggrandisement, and to destructive behaviour towards others and the self.

From this perspective damaged self-esteem is a consequence of an inaccurate, distorted assessment of the self which, because it is inaccurate, provides an invalid basis on which to make decisions. In turn this leads the individual towards attitudes, behaviours and values that create self-harm. Thus, people can have inappropriately low or high self-esteem simply because of a distortion in their understanding of experience or, as is also common, as a defence against perceptions relating to themselves that are too threatening to contemplate. For example, the perception that one is a good enough/OK person may be a perfectly valid and supportive way of viewing oneself. However, if the individual's family has always projected the message only 'the best' is good enough then the reality that one is 'merely OK' is too frightening to acknowledge. The solution to this damaging truth is to come to see and to proclaim oneself as 'the best'.

The relevance of a Person-Centred approach to the self-esteem debate

An examination of the Person-Centred approach to psychological growth may throw light on the sharp disagreements that developed in the debate between Emler's stark view of the relative uselessness of working with self-esteem and Huskin's notion that the concept itself was flawed and too simplistic. It can be argued that the Person-Centred theoretical position demonstrates how hopelessly simplistic are notions of being able to measure self-esteem – for what is being measured will vary with the fluctuations in a person's self-awareness. In one person tests may measure their unconscious defences, in another, their reaction to recent or dominant events in their lives. In addition, the theory demonstrates the complexity of factors that determine people's ways of handling life. Developing an appropriate appreciation of oneself (which we may want to call self-esteem) may be a valuable step on the road to constructive functioning, but it cannot be brought about in isolation. Human beings are, in Huskin's (2002) terms 'holistic entities'. Tinkering with one, albeit complicated aspect of their makeup, cannot be counted upon to bring about the sorts of major changes that we hope to see as an outcome of our work with damaged young people.

For person-centred theorists, change in the client's or pupil's self-concept or structure is one of the main outcomes of a successful, helping relationship. For example, teachers might add here that the development in pupils of a constructive view of themselves is an outcome that they would expect to achieve in a person from a truly pupil-centred school or facilitative educational environment. At first sight it may appear then as if Emler's (2001) findings call into question the fundamental expectations put forward by the Person-Centred approach. Once again, however, the issues of desired aims, objectives and outcomes from a Person-Centred perspective are more complex than Emler's over simplifying, positivist view allows for. For one thing, the Person-Centred helper would not embrace the idea of setting goals (such as an improvement in self-esteem), neither would they devise programmes with those aims in mind. Instead, they would aim to provide specific, facilitative conditions in training or educational environments which, if they were present, would inevitably lead to those outcomes. Indeed, ample research has demonstrated that, where these specific facilitative conditions are provided, changes in client's self concepts do form an aspect of the positive changes that are seen to occur. (Roger, 1951; Bergin & Garfield, 1994; Roth & Fonagy, 1996). So if these changes are not planned for, how do they come about and what changes occur anyway?

How change occurs in Person-Centred approaches

Research over a number of decades has suggested that the major factor that enables positive change to take place is the quality of the relationship established between teacher and pupil, young person and youth worker or, in the therapeutic setting, of the therapeutic alliance established between the therapist and the client (Hovarth & Greenberg, 1986). Given that this holds for any helping relationship this indicates that it is also relevant to work with young people in a variety of personal development settings (Aspy & Roebuck, 1983; Tuasch, 1978; Rogers & Freiberg,1994). Extensive research also suggests that the helper, teacher or therapist must provide core conditions if an intervention is to work (Roger, 1957; Cramer, 1990; Barrett-Lennard, 1981; Orlinskey *et al.*, 1994). Here one wonders how much of the data analysed by Emler (2001) indicated either, whether a therapeutic alliance had been established between programme providers and participants or, whether the core conditions were present on the programme? For if these conditions are not provided, even though the programme design may be excellent, the manner in which it is executed will cause it to fail.

From the Person-Centred perspective the importance of the core conditions is that they not only promote the development of a helping or therapeutic alliance, but that they also provide a generally facilitative climate in which clients can reconnect with their inner sense of what is right for them and rediscover their Actualising Tendency. The aim is to provide a climate that is characterised by specific ways of being on the part of the helper, who seeks to be unconditionally accepting of the client, to demonstrate warmth, liking and appreciation of him or her. In addition, the helper seeks to understand the client's way of viewing the world, as if he or she were the client, and to provide a relationship that, on his or her part, is characterised by authenticity, genuineness and congruence.

So how does the provision of this climate of warmth, empathy and congruence enable the client to change? The answer lies in the fact that, as the client experiences him or herself in a non-judgmental setting, so he or she can begin to let go of the dysfunctional defences and the distorted perceptions that have made it difficult for him or her to choose a constructive path through life. By being received with warmth and appreciation clients feel safe enough to explore and re-examine their perspective on life and themselves. In addition, by being in a congruent, genuine relationship with another, they can begin to hear information about themselves and their world view that is characterised by honesty rather than manipulation or untruths. In such a climate young people can and will make constructive personal changes (Mearns, 1990; Thorne, 1995).

Here it is interesting to note that there is some agreement between Person-Centred predictions and the findings reported not only in Emler's (2001) study, but also in anecdotal evidence produced by other professionals. Namely, all approaches confirm that a warm relationship, with at least one significant other, is found to be a crucial factor in the development of positive self-esteem (*ibid.*).

The changes that occur when a client experiences him or herself in a facilitative helping relationship

Ten significant changes are found to take place as a consequence of the experience of being in what the Person-Centred approach defines as a facilitating relationship. They include three movements away from harmful attitudes or ways of behaving:

Away from:

1. Adopting facades and the constant preoccupation with keeping up appearances.
2. 'Oughts' and an internalised sense of duty springing from externally imposed obligations.
3. Living up to the expectations of others.

They also include seven movements towards constructive attitudes and behaviours:

Towards:

1. Valuing realness and honesty in the self and others.
2. Valuing the capacity to direct one's own life.

3. Accepting and valuing one's self and one's feelings whether they are positive or negative.
4. Valuing the experiences of the moment and the process of growth rather than continually striving for objectives.
5. A greater respect for and understanding of others.
6. A cherishing of close relationships and a longing for more intimacy.
7. A valuing of all forms of intimacy and a willingness to risk being open to all inner and outer experiences however unexpected.

(Thorne, 1996: 121)

These directions of change, which are primarily about rejecting introjected conditions of worth and the search for conditional love, comprise changes to the client's self-structure, components of which will affect a person's self-esteem. Thus, as an individual comes to live more in accordance with his or her own values, and in a way that is more open to experience, his or her self-concept will inevitably change. Clearly these changes are far more complex than might be reflected in the simplicity of such measures as Rosenberg's (1965) self-esteem questionnaire.

Person-Centred practice in outdoor adventure

Outdoor adventure practitioners will make use of the outdoors or adventurous activities because these mediums provide such a powerful setting in which the individual can experience themselves afresh. The novelty or challenge of the outdoor setting provides a fresh space, relatively uncontaminated by past experiences. From a Person-Centred perspective a young person would be joined in that space by a trainer or therapist who resists imposing judgements and conditions of worth on the young person. In this space a Person-Centred outdoor adventure practitioner will work to facilitate the individuals re-examination of him or herself as he or she negotiates the outdoors or the activity, facilitating the client's understanding of the real, personal meaning that these experiences hold. In this way they enable participants to reconnect with a path in life that is truly right for them.

The unique feature of this way of working with young people lies in the fact that it is not based on cajoling or convincing them that by achieving success in challenging activities they can look upon themselves as better people. Instead it is a gentle, reflective approach that provides the setting for a collaborative enquiry out of which young people can come to understand, respect and appreciate themselves. Consequently, encouragement, instruction and confrontation play a far smaller part in the person-centred outdoor practitioner's approach than they do in other traditional outdoor facilitators' work – for they are seen as crowding out the space in which young people might be able to listen to him or herself. Where they are present, they spring naturally from the warmth, congruence and unconditionally accepting nature of the practitioner's relationship with his or her client and are provided merely to complement the client's growing self-understanding.

Conclusion

It can be argued that such an approach, which works at a far greater depth than mere tinkering with self-esteem, offers a new way of thinking about the relationships that helpers have to establish with the damaged young people with whom they are working. It calls for a deeper level of understanding of the processes that cause damage to young people and an acknowledgement of the real hard work of relating that is needed to produce healing and constructive change.

References

Aspy, D., & Reobuck, F. N. (1978). Researching person-centred issues in education. In C.R. Rogers (Ed.), *Freedom to learn in the '80s* (pp. 199-217). Columbus, OH: Charles Merrill.

Barrett-Lennard, G.T. (1986). The relationship inventory now: Issues and advances in theory, method and use. In L. S. Greenberg & W. M. Pinsof (Eds.), *The psychotherapeutic process: A research handbook* (pp. 439-76). New York: Guildford Press.

Bergin, A., & Garfield, S. (Eds.) (1994). *Handbook of psychotherapy and behavioural change* (4th edition). New York: Wiley.

Cramer, D. (1990). The necessary conditions for evaluating client centred therapy. In G. Lietaer., J. Rombaults & R. Van Balen (Eds.), *Client centred and experiential therapies in the nineties* (pp. 415-28). Leuven: University of Leuvens Press.

Emler, N. (2001). *Self-esteem: The costs and causes of low self-worth*. York: Joseph Rowntree Foundation / YPS.

Hovarth, A.O., & Greenberg, L.S. (1986). Development and validation of the working alliance inventory. *Journal of Counselling Psychology*, 36: 223-33.

Huskins, J. (2002). *Self-esteem and youth development*. Paper presented at Self-esteem and Youth Development Seminar, 29 April, Brathay Hall Trust, London.

Mearns, D. (1990). The counsellor's experience of success. In D. Mearns & W. Dryden, (Eds.), *Experiences of counselling in action* (pp. 97-112). London: Sage.

Orlinsky, D.E., Grawe, K., & Parks, B.K. (1994). Process and outcome in psychotherapy. In A. Bergin & S. Garfield (Eds.), *Handbook of psychotherapy and behavioural change* (pp. 270-376). New York: Wiley.

Rogers, C. R. (1951). *Client-centred therapy*. Boston: Houghton Miffin.

Rogers, C. R. (1957). The necessary and sufficient conditions of therapeutic personality change. *Journal of Counselling Psychology*, 21: 95-104.

Rogers, C. R., & Freiberg, J. (1994). *Freedom to learn*. Canada: MacMillan.

Rosenberg, M. (1965). *Society and the adolescent self-image*. Princeton, NJ: Princeton University Press.

Roth, A., & Fonagy, P. (1996). *What works for whom? A critical review of psychotherapy research*. New York: Guildford Press.

Tausk, R. (1978). Facilitative dimensions in interpersonal relation: Verifying the theoretical assumptions of Carl Rogers in School, family education, client-centred therapy and encounter groups. *College Student Journal*, 12: 2-12.

Thorne, B. (1996). Person-centred therapy. In W. Dryden (Ed.), *Handbook of individual therapy* (pp. 66-87). London: Sage Publications.

Thorne, B. (1992). *Carl Rogers*. London: Sage Publications.

Author Biography

Dr Jenny Peel is Principal Lecturer in Education Studies at Liverpool John Moores University. She has worked as a psychotherapist for twenty years in both private practice and as a counsellor trainer. Before that she worked in youth work and as a school teacher. At present she is Director of Studies for the research project (conducted by Kaye Richards) on Adventure Therapy and Eating Disorders (*see* this volume) and runs Adventure Therapy training modules at undergraduate and postgraduate levels.

Insights from practice: youth development and self-esteem

Alison Butcher

Introduction

The evolution of our society, filled with uncertainty, challenge and change, has made the importance of raising self-esteem and developing complementary attributes in young people more critical than ever before. Britain and indeed much of the western world has bred a culture whereby image and surface appearance have overtaken matters of substance and meaning in defining the lives of young people. The complexities of adolescence make it difficult for young people to access the support structures that offer care and guidance to help them gain a deeper sense of themselves and understanding of their identities. Gone are the many 'rites of passage' that previously marked and recognised important transitions, enabling young people to value themselves and to be recognised and valued by the larger community.

As pointed out by Lewis (2002), those in the employment sector recognise that times have changed and that we need to adapt and nurture a different skill set from those merely associated with academic qualifications:

> When we talk about the kind of economy that we want in the future, increasingly employers say well we have more young people coming out of the education system with higher levels of qualifications than historically, but on many occasions they don't have the skills like leadership, inter-personal skills, communication skills and teamwork skills that are absolutely essential in a modern labour market and a modern economy.

Yet, despite the ever-changing economic position of society a large proportion of young people's success, as gauged by the wider community, still rests on academic ability within the formal education

LIVERPOOL JOHN MOORES UNIVERSITY
LEARNING SERVICES

system. A sense of self-worth can all too easily be based upon an individual's prowess at the passing of examinations and progression to further education or employment. While some young people thrive in this environment, what of those who do not? What impact does an emphasis on achievement as valued by others have on their self-perception? Further, how are we as youth practitioners equipping young people not just to survive, but more importantly to thrive in everyday life in ways that meet their own developmental needs?

The transition from youth to adulthood is not just about being able to earn a living. It is also about:

- being grounded and happy with one's sense of self.
- exploring individual creativity and vision for one's role in the world.
- seeking out and being given responsibility.
- feeling a sense of place and belonging in the wider community.
- and having the skills and confidence to question and challenge the world.

However, the reality of adolescence for a lot of young people is diametrically opposed to the ideal – many young people genuinely think that they cannot alter their own lives, let alone have a positive impact upon society. They feel alienated and disempowered, constantly receiving mixed messages from adults, the media, schools, youth agencies and the home environment. So why in a bid to counteract these mixed messages of self-worth and to empower young people to believe that they can make a difference in the world is the raising of self-esteem seen as the answer to all? This is a question we need to critically reflect upon in our practice as youth workers.

The practice of working with young people

Many national youth initiatives have identified the raising of self-esteem as a key objective for programmes. In collaborating with partners on the design of experiential learning programmes for young people it appears almost as a prerequisite. However, the development of self-esteem is not a process in isolation, it is one developmental aim of several desired skills or attributes.

The Summer Activities Initiatives for 16 years olds, now known as the 'u-Project' and funded by The New Opportunities Fund, is currently in its fourth year of implementation. The programme, which was established under the banner of "raising aspirations in the 21st century" (DfEE, 2000), aims to help young people feel empowered in the transition from school to further education training or employment. The objectives for young people who participate on the programme are:

- to develop self-esteem.
- to develop confidence.
- to develop teamwork.
- to develop leadership skills.
- to broaden horizons.

The national evaluations of the 'u-Project' (SQW, 2003) and peer research run by young people to evaluate the 'u-Project' in Cumbria reported improvement in self-esteem and self-confidence for young people participating in these programmes. In particular, the peer research project run in Cumbria highlighted that a raised self-esteem was identified by some of the participants as a positive outcome, almost to the exclusion of the other objectives (Richards, 2002). This raises relevant questions to the self-esteem debate. For example, did the young people involved in the project not get the opportunities during the residential experiences to take on a leadership role or develop teamwork skills? Or, did they not see those skills as relevant to their current perspective on life? Or, is there a foundation level of confidence and self-esteem needed before some individuals can begin to work in other areas. Or, does success in another area in fact impact upon feelings of self-worth? These are interesting questions in trying to assess the role and function of self-esteem in relation to young people's developmental processes. A rise in self-esteem is certainly a statistic of note but what is the reality of that for the young person concerned? How do I as a practitioner know the objective has been achieved and what is the longevity of such a transition?

Young people's experiences

As Emler (2001) highlights in his research report, the raising of self-esteem is often trumpeted as a divergent from drugs, teenage pregnancy and crime in disaffected youth. In the context of this debate I want to ask about the less dramatic and, yet, perhaps numerically large impacts for those young people who do not fit the categories as defined previously? For example, the young man changing college courses because, despite parental disapproval, painting and decorating is not for him. Also, the young carer who can stand up in front of care agency staff and recognise and value the skills and qualities she has both in her role as carer for her disabled mother and as an individual in her own right. Neither of these will alter government statistics in any way, but have an impact for those individuals concerned.

In trying to recognise the ways in which young people give meaning to their own lives and to give evidence to what we as youth workers may intuitively consider as impacts upon self-esteem I will share two different stories. These stories will not provide a detailed analysis and evaluation of self-esteem theory in relation to them, however, they may give some insight into the meaningful processes of change that I and other youth workers observe in the lives of young people we work with. This enables us to reconsider what we may or may not mean about the processes and practices of self-esteem enhancement in practice.

A young woman moving towards change

I recall a young woman on a seven-day residential development training programme who, although partially engaged in the course, was prone to turbulent mood-swings and self-doubt about what she herself could achieve and contribute to the group. Things came to a head half way through the programme when the young woman concerned opened up to the group about abuse she had experienced earlier in her childhood. She expressed the difficulty she was having dealing with this, along with living and working intensely with a group of relative strangers in a residential environment. Options were explored to offer additional support and to make sure this was followed up at the end of the residential programme, but it never crossed her mind to leave the course.

By the end of the week she had become much more relaxed and happy within herself, which showed in her posture, her engagement with her peers, her involvement in activities and the very fact that at the end of the course she volunteered to be photographed and interviewed. Being photographed and interviewed was a personal risk for her to take, she had spent the week covering her mouth whenever she spoke, turning away and hiding her face whenever a camera was used.

Since the end of the programme I have had contact with this young woman four times. The first was a phone call from her to let me know that she was about to start a programme of counselling and that she had never experienced anything like the Summer Activities Initiative programme. She also commented on the "amazing relationships" that had developed between her and the other young people on the course. Even though it had been hard for her and she felt that she had behaved like a "complete pain in the arse" at times, it was the most "fantastic thing" she had ever experienced or achieved.

The second time I spoke to her was at a celebration evening where young people who had participated on a variety of Summer Activity Initiative programmes in Cumbria were awarded certificates and celebrated their successes. The whole group turned up early and could not stop talking about their experiences to whoever would listen. They spoke of how, of course, they were the best group, of what they had achieved, and of how most of them had kept in contact with each other and that in fact they were "all round superstars". By the end of the evening, when the time came to clear away, the group was still talking, was energetic and almost had to be thrown out into the night.

The third time I had contact with her was a phone call to say that she had been arrested for assaulting a police officer and would be appearing at court the following week. My final contact with her came in a letter from her letting me know she was attending an anger management programme as a result of the previous incident and had applied to go on a training course saying "I know that I can stick at it because of all the stuff I did in the summer".

For me the unravelling of her story is part of the reality of a woolly statistic regarding the building of what might be termed as the self-esteem of a young woman. She was one of seven young people whose individual growth over the course of a week was evident. To you or me they may not seem huge changes, but in relative terms many are important first steps in an ongoing process of enabling young people to gain a sense of self-worth.

A group of young carers expressing their appreciation of themselves

I recently worked on a drama programme with a group of young carers, one as young as 12 years old, who have the primary responsibility of caring for a disabled or ill parent, and some who also care for their younger siblings. The young people had only met once before the programme and the aim of the programme was to develop a piece of theatre about life as a young carer. This would then be performed to a group of support service professionals at an awareness-raising conference. The young people's contribution to this conference was part of a longer-term developmental programme. The aim of this programme was to support the young people in building a peer support network, to explore opportunities to make changes in their lives, and, more importantly for them, to validate their experiences of being young carers and individuals in their own right.

On arrival at the residential programme several of the group members were withdrawn, unwilling to talk with others and very hesitant to take part in warm-up activities. Slowly conversation developed, the focus of which was how proud they were of the person they cared for, what they were going or had gone through (one young man had recently lost his mother) and how sometimes they felt hopeless or inadequate in trying to be there for them. For the young people involved it was easier to be proud of someone else than to identify or admit to themselves their own strengths and skills. Many of the group said that they found it hard to make friends because they could not join in activities after school or at lunch times when they might have to do errands for those at home. Often they were behind on their homework and were afraid of disclosing the reason for fear of being bullied.

A real turning point for the group came during a session when they explored all the requests that might be made on them during a 24-hour period and the consequences for them as a result. They were shocked at the level of what they did – seeing it mapped out in front of them had a real impact. There was much commonality within their situations and the young people started to share their histories and talk about their responsibilities. Over the rest of the weekend through role-play and creative expression, the young people grew in stature and re-framed their perspective on their lives, wanting to share their views with others.

Before they left the residential programme it was suggested to the group that they might want to take part in an informal question and answers session during the lunch break. They reluctantly agreed. Two weeks later, on the morning of the conference, I was approached by a deputation who now not only very clearly wanted to answer questions, but also wanted to do so on stage as part of their performance.

To see the group on stage performing to 150 people and afterwards answering questions was very humbling for me. The group was at the front of the stage clearly saying,

> This is me! Here I am and I'm proud! I am proud of my family and my role in it. I don't need the acknowledgement of the paid carer who sometimes arrives in the morning expecting me to go back into the role of the child, when it's me who has been sat up comforting Mum all night. I am proud of who I am beyond my role as carer and what I have to offer the world as an individual in my own right.

If, as I believe, what I saw, felt and heard was indeed a positive impact on self-worth for the young people involved, how can I isolate the contributory factors and design a learning environment that allows young people to experience their uniqueness and build on their own inner sense of dignity in a sustainable way?

Developing a positive environment for young people

In designing a development training programme for young people one of the first issues to be explored is what is the quality and relevance of the programme for the young people involved? It is important for the trainers and youth workers not to set themselves up as experts in relation to young people. We need to allow real empowerment and ownership of a programme within the boundaries of safe practice.

Our ownership of and acceptance in space and territory impacts on how we see our self-worth in society. Inclusion or exclusion from peer, social groups and places can deeply affect how we define ourselves. It is important for a practitioner to create an environment that is inclusive and supportive, both emotionally and physically, whilst at the same time providing a challenging and stimulating learning environment. Creating such an environment of inclusiveness is not always easy, when we ourselves are influenced in our interactions with young people by our own prejudices, preferences and life experience.

Tucker (2003) suggests that the whole relationship between the young people and the training staff is a fundamental element of a successful programme. The fostering of unconditional positive regard between both staff and peers is deeply significant. Those attending the Summer Activities Initiative peer evaluation weekend, as referred to earlier, echoed these findings. A fundamental issue impacting on the outcomes from their experience was whether the training staff used a consistent approach.

The young people who actively sought responsibility within the programmes were met with differing experiences. For example, one young person commented, "the staff were great they were like young old people, listening to us. We made the choices but we knew they were there for us". So the young person whose experience was positive had felt valued, and he or she was able to recognise the importance of having the opportunity to both make decisions and to be directly responsible for the consequences of those choices, personally and for others. However, the young people whose contact with training staff was not always so consistent felt it reflected many of the conflicting attitudes experienced in their everyday lives. As commented by one young person, "they expected us to behave like adults but treated us like kids". As these young people continued to talk further about these experiences they started to air frustrations. They questioned how a society allows a 16-year-old to make the decision to create another life, yet cannot appear to value their opinions enough to enable them to create the society in which that child will be raised. This represents some of the mixed messages young people receive in their experiences of negotiating the transition from youth to adulthood. It raises questions as to how we value young people as adults, and what impact this has on the difficult task of sustaining a sense of self-worth in a changing world.

Affirming young people's experiences

It is hugely important for an individual to be recognised and respected for who they are, where they have come from and not just what they might become. Looking backwards and validating what past experiences young people have of the world is an important ingredient, yet risks being overlooked as we work towards achieving the outcomes of development training programmes. In working with young people on personal development programmes, allowing space and time for their stories to be heard is significant. This allows individuals to generate an understanding and appreciation of themselves not just based on the here and now of activities, but by drawing on their life experiences to date. Informal discussions around a fire, a night walk through a forest, quiet time on a lakeshore have all created a safe space to enable continued sharing and learning from past experience and the exploration of self. It is sometimes too easy to cram a programme with activity, review and transfer to the future and not allow quality time for acknowledging past achievements and experiences.

Whatever the content in terms of activity and the vehicle for learning on programmes, important elements include the opportunity for discovery through adventure and challenge and the experience of success for individuals involved. However, in the increasingly escalated transition from youth to adulthood, opportunities are lost for learning through the freedom of play and experimentation in an environment where those around create a buffer for the consequences of choices. Young people find themselves in an arena that all too often views success and failure in terms of either/or, promoting in some individuals a hesitancy to take risks or to grasp opportunities in their everyday lives for fear of failure. Creating opportunities whereby success is more subjective for the individual concerned and enabling young people to recognise and celebrate their own skills and qualities is surely fundamental in the development of self-awareness and the raising of self-esteem. It will enable the creation of an understanding that we make the right choices based on the information we have available to us at that time, but that these might not be the right decisions for us a day, a week, or a month down the line, but that is acceptable.

If indeed we can increase an individual's self-esteem how do we know that it is sustainable? What happens when a young person returns home at the end of the residential programme? Have we equipped them with the tools to implement the attributes they may have developed for future use? How do we know whether, and in what form, the impact of an experience will manifest itself? What is important to recognise is that we need to look beyond the initial stimulus. Residential programmes need to be structured with follow-up in school, home or the community and for evaluation to be an on-going process. This is important to ensure that young people are not set up to fail: it is all too easy to empower young people whilst they are away from their everyday environment only for them to then find themselves back in an environment where repeating patterns of disempowerment continue to be fed.

Conclusion

As a practitioner, what I reflect upon is based on my own observation and perceptions taken from 15 privileged years of working with young people. In the continuing debate surrounding the raising of self-esteem, its success and long-term implications, I am not suggesting that there is no value in the research and evaluation of the work we do. Indeed, we should constantly be questioning what we are doing, with whom and why, and seeking out and sharing best practice. Yet, let's keep it really fresh and alive. As practitioners we may not be sophisticated enough to capture the complexities, the impact or measured signs of developing self-esteem, and it may be that young adults do not articulate this in a way that we as adults have defined as significant. However, in the name of research let us not miss out or invalidate the voices of young people, the passion and richness of their stories, and the value of the ever-evolving process of youth work.

References

DfEE (2000). *Invitation to Tender (ITT) for Summer Activities for 16 Year Olds – Pilot Programmes in 2001*. London: DfEE.

Emler, N. (2001). *Self-esteem: The costs and causes of low self-worth*. York: Joseph Rowntree Foundation / YPS.

Lewis, I. (2002). Paper presented at *Transforming youth work. Resourcing Excellent Youth Services Conference*, 18 December, Business Design Centre, Islington, London.

Richards, K. (2002). *Summer activities for 16 year olds. An initial evaluation report*. Brathay: Unpublished internal report.

SQW. (2003). Evaluation of the activities for young people initiative. First year interim report. London: SQW Limited.

Tucker, N. (2003). Participants' and practitioners' experience of outdoor experiential personal and social development. In B. Humberstone, H. Brown, and K. Richards (Eds.), *Whose journeys? The outdoors and adventure as social and cultural phenomena. Critical explorations between individuals, 'others' and the environment* (pp. 273-288). Cumbria: The Institute for Outdoor Learning.

Author Biography

Alison Butcher is a qualified teacher with 15 years' youth work experience. Her work has a strong emphasis on facilitating purposeful experiences for young people in the outdoors. Alison is currently Team Leader in the Youth Team at Brathay, where she has a keen interest in developing creative and environmental projects for youth development.

Self-esteem in youth work policy and practice

Steve Lenartowicz

Introduction

In his research for the Joseph Rowntree Foundation Emler (2001) points out that raising young people's self-esteem has frequently come to be seen as a panacea for a wide range of personal and social issues. However, he demonstrates that there is little research evidence for such an assumption. How has this situation come about? What is the connection between self-esteem, young people's development and the national agenda in education and youth work?

Policy and youth work

In recent years, three key issues have emerged in the debate about national priorities for policies that affect young people's education and development. They are social inclusion, citizenship and employability.

Social inclusion

In his introduction to Excellence in Schools (DfEE, 1997), David Blunkett, then Secretary of State for Education and Employment, outlined five priorities for education, of which the first two were about social inclusion:

- the need to overcome economic and social disadvantages.
- the creation of greater fairness within the education system.

One of the first actions of the incoming Labour government in 1997 was to set up the Social Exclusion Unit. The Prime Minister, Tony Blair, introduced the Unit's report on preventing social exclusion by highlighting what he saw as a deep social crisis.

> ...sharp income inequality, a third of children growing up in poverty, a host of social problems such as homelessness and drug abuse, and divisions in society typified by deprived neighbourhoods that had become no-go areas for some and no-exit zones for others. (Cabinet Office, 2001: 4)

A key issue identified in the Social Exclusion Unit's seminal report *Bridging the Gap* (Social Exclusion Unit, 1999) was the fact that a large number of young people drop out of education at the age of 16, having completed compulsory schooling. Addressing this problem has become fundamental to the government's strategy.

The issue of youth offending has been seen as both a result and as a cause of social exclusion. *Bridging the Gap* (*ibid.*) cited young people involved in offending as one of the groups at particular risk of social exclusion. Research by the Audit Commission (1996) identified that young people in certain circumstances are at much greater risk of falling into a cycle of antisocial behaviour including offending. These circumstances include inadequate parenting, truancy and exclusion from school and lack of training and employment. The Government's response to these problems has been to attempt to put in place a number of broad strategies to encourage 'joined-up thinking'. As well as the Social Exclusion Unit, these include the introduction of the cross-departmental Children and Young People's Unit, and initiatives such as *Sure Start* for 0–4 year-olds, the Children's Fund for preventative work with 5-13 year olds, and the Connexions Service, which aims at a single, coherent service aimed at all 13–19 year olds.

Citizenship

There has been rising concern over what has been termed the 'democratic deficit'. It is estimated that only 39% of 18–24 year olds voted in the 2001 general election (MORI, 2001). The Industrial Society's 2020 Vision project found that only one-fifth of young people said that they felt part of their community, and very few actively participated in local or national politics (Industrial Society, 1997).

Much debate has taken place around the concept of 'active citizenship'. Hall and Williamson (1999) see this as representing a shift away from passive notions of citizenship based on rights, towards a notion of citizenship based on community, participation and respon-sibility. In making proposals for the introduction of citizenship into the National Curriculum – which happened in September 2002 – the Qualifications and Curriculum Authority argues that this will enable young people "to participate in society as active citizens of our democracy" (QCA / DfEE, 1999: 28). These proposals are based on the *Crick Report* (QCA, 1998), which saw citizenship as being composed of three interdependent strands: social and moral responsibility, community involvement and political literacy.

Employability

The fast-changing nature of society has given rise to increasing concerns that our present education system does not adequately prepare young people for the world of work. Employers are demanding a workforce that is highly skilled, flexible and able to cope with change. Research by Industry in Education found that the lack of 'employability qualities' might be costing Britain £8 billion or more each year (Industry in Education, 1996). It found that employers increasingly prefer to recruit older and more experienced members of the workforce, rather than young people. A further report (Industry in Education, 2001) revealed similar concerns about the employability of graduates. The British Chamber of Commerce (BCC, 1998) identified a rising skills shortage in industry, and felt that the most important reason for this is a lack of employability skills in young people.

Addressing the policy issues in youth work practice

Much attention has been given to addressing these three issues. It is noteworthy that a common theme has emerged among the conclusions. It is this: that if we are to build a society which is inclusive, in which all people participate as active citizens, and which is economically successful, then we must give much more attention to the development of young people's personal attributes, attitudes and social skills.

Research into young people's employability (Anderson Consulting, 1998: 10) concluded that, "the best passport to employment for young people is a specific bundle of attributes". Among these attributes it not only identified the key skills of communication, working with others, improving own learning and performance, problem-solving, numeracy and information technology, but also vital attitudes such as enthusiasm, initiative, honesty, commitment, positiveness, adaptability, flexibility and willingness to work. This research confirmed the findings of Industry in Education (1996), which argued for a shift of emphasis from skills to personal qualities, and of the Confederation of British Industry (CBI, 1998), which recommended that the curriculum should support the development of values and attitudes.

Tom Bentley (1998), of the influential think-tank Demos, argues along comparable lines regarding employability, identifying generic transferable abilities such as orientation to change, interpersonal skills, analytical skills and problem solving. He also addresses the issue of active citizenship, and comes to the conclusion that similar generic personal attributes are involved. He particularly highlights the concept of trust, arguing that young people show markedly lower levels of 'social trust' as well as trust in institutions, than do older age groups. The theme of trust as a basis for society was picked up by Onora O'Neill in the 2002 BBC Reith Lectures (O'Neill 2002), where she examined its fundamental role in the functioning of society.

Merton and Parrott (1999) use examples of successful practice in educational work with disaffected young adults to argue that a curriculum focus on attitudes and attributes, as opposed to knowledge and skills, is necessary for social inclusion as well as employability.

Picking up on this theme, recent education policy documents have introduced the concept of 'education with character'. In her introduction to the recent consultation on the 14–19 curriculum (DfES, 2002), the then Education Secretary, Estelle Morris, identified the promotion of 'education with character' as one of the four central challenges that our country must address if we are to guarantee economic prosperity and social justice. The term was first used in an earlier education Green Paper (DfEE, 2001a), where it was described as an approach that helps young people to: develop the skills, attitudes and habits of mind which enable them to know right from wrong; to get along with others; to work in teams; to make a contribution to the school as a community; and to develop positive attitudes to life and work. These were linked with the need to increase self-esteem and confidence. A major report from the National Advisory Committee on Creative and Cultural Education (DfEE, 1999) also argues strongly for promoting young people's motivation, self-esteem, skills and aptitudes in order to develop creativity, adaptability and better powers of communication

In parallel with these educational policies, which tend to be school-focused, there is currently much debate about the role of youth work and youth services. In its strategy for transforming youth work (DfEE, 2001b), the government identifies young people's personal, social and educational development as the first priority of youth work, describing this as keeping young people in 'good shape'. In a case study of good practice, it states that young people cannot achieve their goals in education or employment "without first increasing their self-esteem and changing their behaviour and attitudes" (DfEE, 2001b: 11).

The role of self-esteem in youth work policy and practice

Although self-esteem is occasionally mentioned in the many policy documents, it is seen as only one of a range of attributes needed by young people. This is also the case within the field of youth work. For example, the National Youth Agency (NYA, 2002) describes the main outcomes of youth work as being that young people:

- Gain confidence and self-esteem while having fun and socialising with their peers.
- Develop new skills and interests through group activities.
- Increase their knowledge and understanding of issues affecting their lives.
- Develop planning, organisation and teamwork skills through active participation.
- Learn how to make use of services and information to make informed choices about their lives.
- Gain greater control over their lives through access to education and training tailored to their needs.

John Huskins (*see* this volume) places self-esteem in a framework of personal qualities and social skills and argues persuasively about how these can be most effectively developed within a progressive and empowering programme of youth work activities.

Despite the fact that, at policy level, self-esteem is not given a particularly high profile above other personal attributes, in practice it often seems to emerge prominently. For example, one government initiative has been the launch of a summer programme of activities for 16-year-olds, branded as the 'u-Project'. This aims to provide a programme of personal development in order to motivate them to re-engage with education or training. The building of self-esteem and confidence is identified as just one of a number of activities that may be included, and is not identified as one of the key objectives (New Opportunities Fund, 2001). Yet, a major article on the programme in the *Financial Times* (14th May 2002) was headlined 'Summer School for Self Esteem'.

In a recent article in the youth work press, White (2002) argues that many youth work projects have used self-esteem as a 'catch-all' description of their work. They have not undertaken an in-depth analysis of the needs of the young people they work with, nor have they thought through exactly what they mean by self-esteem. This uncritical approach has meant that youth work is open to criticism as weak, intuitive, vague and impressionistic, rather than robust and testable.

Conclusion

Clearly, the concept of self-esteem has relevance to young people's development, and therefore to wider policy issues in youth work and education. However, Emler's (2001) work has alerted us to the fact that there is currently much lack of clarity around the subject. It will only be by examining closely what we really mean by the term 'self-esteem', how we observe and measure it, what are the causes and costs of its absence, and how it is developed to its optimum level, that we will clarify matters. Otherwise, we are in danger of basing our policy and practice on woolly thinking rather than evidence and informed professional judgement.

References

Audit Commission. (1996). *Misspent youth: Young people and crime*. London: Audit Commission.

Bentley, T. (1998). *Learning beyond the classroom*. London: Routledge.

Cabinet Office. (2001). *Preventing social exclusion*. London: Social Exclusion Unit.

CBI. (1998). *Human resources brief: Greater expectations. Priorities for the future curriculum*. British Chamber of Commerce (BBC, 1998).

DfEE. (1997). *Excellence in schools*. London: HMSO.

DfEE. (1999). *All our futures: Creativity, culture and education*. Sudbury, Suffolk: DfEE Publications.

DfEE. (2001a). *Schools: Building on success*. Norwich: The Stationery Office.

DfEE. (2001b). *Transforming youth work*. Nottingham: DfEE Publications.

DfES. (2002). *14-19: Extending opportunities, raising standards*. Norwich: The Stationery Office.

Emler, N. (2001). *Self-esteem. The costs and causes of low self-worth*. York: York Publishing Services.

Hall, T., & Williamson, W. (1999). *Citizenship and community*. Leicester: Youth Work Press.

Industrial Society. (1997). *Speaking up speaking out!* London: The Industrial Society.

Industry in Education. (2001). *Graduates' employability skills*. Radlett, Hertfordshire: Industry in Education.

Industry in Education. (1996). *Towards employability*. London: Industry in Education.

Merton, B. & Parrott, A. (1999). *Only connect*. Leicester: NIACE.

MORI. (2001). Survey of attitudes during the 2001 General Election campaign. http//mori.com/polls/2001/elec_comm_rep.shtml

New Opportunities Fund. (2001). *Activities for young people: Guidance notes*. NYA. http://www.nya.org.uk/YS-whatis.htm

NYA. (2002). *Pledging the future. Annual Report 2002-2003*. Leicester: The National Youth Agency.

O'Neill, O. (2002). A question of trust. http://www.bbc.co.uk/radio4/reith2002/

QCA (1998). *Education for citizenship and the teaching of democracy in schools*. London: Qualifications and Curriculum Authority.

QCA / DfEE. (1999). *The review of the national curriculum in England: The Secretary of State's proposals*. London: Qualifications and Curriculum Authority.

Social Exclusion Unit. (1999). *Bridging the gap: New opportunities for 16-18 year olds not in education, training or employment*. London: The Stationery Office.

White, P. J. (2002). Steamed up about self-esteem. *Young People Now*, 162: 24-25.

Author Biography

Steve Lenartowicz is currently Youth Development Director at Brathay, where he also heads the Brathay Academy. He has worked as a teacher in an inner-city comprehensive school in Manchester, as a tutor in a number of outdoor education and development training centres, and in teacher-training with VSO. He is a trustee of the Institute for Outdoor Learning.

No strings attached: the challenge of detaching ourselves from 'outcomes' in work with young people

Barbara Smith

Introduction

As a psychotherapist and former social worker, who has worked with children for over twenty years, most of my professional contact with children and young people has been with those who are either in some kind of emotional distress or whose behaviour is causing distress in the adults around them. I am mindful of Emler's (2001: 60-61) comment, "the efforts to raise self-esteem represented by so many programmes, projects and therapies are not driven primarily by the belief that high self-esteem is desirable in it's own right. Rather, it is to be desired because of the benefits it delivers". I believe that it is this very phenomenon – our strong focus on changing children, often for the benefit of others – which sabotages the success of much 'self-esteem work'.

I take the title for this chapter from a quote from Berne and Savary (2000: 35), "when relating to children, especially when they feel threatened, let them know they do not have to prove themselves to you. Let them know there are no strings attached to what you do or to what you ask them to do". When we adults attach ourselves too strongly and focus too closely on behavioural outcomes then we fall into the trap of missing the relational opportunities offered in process work which is fundamental to enhancing esteem.

Acceptance

My own philosophy is that if we give love and attention to the child *as he/she is right now* then, over time, behavioural changes will emerge. If they don't, then so be it. You have given the child love and attention. This is in keeping with the work of Carl Rogers (1951), the parent of

Person-Centred Therapy, who puts the relationship between client and therapist at the heart of therapeutic work. Elsewhere in this text, Jennifer Peel has given us a chapter on the importance of acceptance in self-esteem work, one of the fundamental concepts of Rogers' theory. In his discussion of self-esteem, Mruk (1999: 60) highlights the relationship between self-esteem and acceptance.

> In regard to self-esteem, being accepted means that significant others value us as worthy of their time and attention... It is important to realize that there are many ways that acceptance and rejection may be alive in relation to the development and maintenance of self-esteem. For instance, care, nurturance and attraction are important features of acceptance, but respect, fondness and admiration are more appropriate in a work or professional relationship.

I will highlight the importance of the distinction between acceptance for *being* and acceptance for *doing*, in my discussion on the concept of *strokes* from Transactional Analysis Psychotherapy; simple in its application, but complex in terms of human motivational theory. I will explain how I use 'stroking' in my practice with young people, exploring the process and highlighting some of the interesting changes that emerge. We are not talking here about stroking in the usual physical sense of the word (although physical contact is still a stroke).

Strokes

Berne (1961) defined a transaction of recognition as a 'stroke'. He suggests that the need for strokes (or stimulus) is what motivates us to behave in certain ways in our relationships with others. There are different kinds of strokes. Some are *positive strokes*, which generally feel pleasant to receive and others *negative strokes* which feel unpleasant. Some are *conditional strokes* "I like you when you smile" – the liking is conditional on smiling, and others are *unconditional strokes* "I like you" – there are no conditions to the liking. I think of unconditional strokes as strokes for *being* and conditional strokes as strokes for *doing*. Strokes can be *verbal* "It's really good to see you" or *non-verbal* such as a hug or a smile.

Let us take the example of a classroom full of children with their teacher. The teacher might greet James with a smile. This is a *non-verbal, positive, unconditional stroke*. James gets positive recognition simply for being. He doesn't have to do anything; just his very being is enough. Similarly, Angelica might be met with "Hello Angelica" as she arrives to school. This is a *verbal, positive, unconditional stroke*. Rachel may have produced a piece of homework that was overdue. The teacher might say "Oh well done Rachel, you've managed to do the work". This is a *positive, conditional stroke* for doing. This encourages Rachel to produce homework in the future. She feels esteemed by her teacher and can internalise this esteem – "If this important adult thinks I'm OK then I must be". Alternatively the teacher may say sarcastically to Rachel "Oh you've finally decided to do some work". This *negative conditional stroke* produces feelings of shame and rejection in Rachel. She is only esteemed if she produces her work on time. Even more rejecting is the *negative unconditional stroke*. Damien walks into the classroom and the teacher says coldly "And what delights have you got in store for us today Smith?" Damien's very being evokes a hostile, negative reaction in the teacher.

"Negative strokes are better than no strokes at all"

Interestingly, although most people experience negative strokes as unpleasant, some continue to engage in behaviours that will elicit these unpleasant negative strokes from other people. Take, for example children who, despite sanctions and alienation by others, continue to behave in ways which are anti-social and which do not help them. The hunger for recognition or 'being seen' is so great, that strokes of any kind are preferable to being ignored. Just as being deprived of water or food motivates vigorous activity to restore them, the need for recognition or 'stroke hunger' motivates us to seek recognition. Steiner (2000: 6) suggests, "we will pursue them [strokes] hungrily and if we can't get the good ones we'll settle for bad ones". He likens taking negative strokes to drinking polluted water. "Extreme need will cause us to overlook the harmful qualities of what we require to survive" (Steiner, 1974: 107). Being ignored leaves us unsure of who we are, lonely and abandoned. Research has shown that strokes are required for *actual* survival in young children (Spitz, 1945, cited in Clarkson, 1992: 15), and psychological survival and health in adults. Often, when adult clients first come for therapy, they may talk about their confusion about why they have come; confused about their problems or feelings of distress or lack of fulfilment. They talk of having had two good parents who fed them, clothed them, and took them on holidays every year. They never wanted for anything. They were not beaten or abused in any way. Invariably, on further exploration, we learn about the 'drip drip' effect of being left alone, ignored, and left to 'get on with it'. Emotional abandonment can leave terrible scars that can take a long time to heal in the therapeutic relationship.

The stroke economy

Steiner (1974) suggests that we live by a set of rules that he calls 'the stroke economy'. He tells us of a set of five 'rules' which have been imposed upon us by society and which limit our capacity to grow. These 'stroke economy' rules are:

- don't give strokes you want to give.
- don't accept strokes you want to get.
- don't ask for strokes you need.
- don't reject strokes you dislike.
- don't give yourself strokes.

In the late 1960s, he established, with others, the 'RAP Center' in Berkely, which stood for 'Radical Approach to Psychiatry'. One of the groups to emerge from this was what they called 'Stroke City'. The work of Stroke City was to turn these rules on their heads; to teach people how to give and receive positive strokes, how to ask for the strokes they needed and how to refuse the negative strokes they did not want. They learned how to give themselves positive strokes and to recognise and enjoy their positive qualities. Steiner (2003: 9) describes what emerged from the work.

What had started as an exercise to practise how to be cooperative and positive towards others turned out to affect the participants' loving capacities in a powerful and heart expanding way. It was then that we began to see the connection between strokes and love.

Teaching the art of stroking

About twenty years ago, whilst working for a local authority as a social worker in a children and families team, I became interested in assertiveness training. In my enthusiasm, nobody escaped the offer of assertiveness training by myself with one or two colleagues. We worked with young people leaving care, social workers, youth justice workers, foster carers – anyone who'd show an interest in our work – but the most memorable were a group of women who were lone parents and whose young children were on the Child Protection Register. As workers, we were expecting to help them to make assertive requests to other agencies such as the Housing Department, DSS, etc.; to explore their rights and responsibilities as citizens and to help them to empower themselves generally in their dealings with others. What transpired was that these women were well practiced at dealing with Housing Officers and ensuring that they received their due benefits. What they could not do was tell their children that they loved them. The expression of positive emotion was difficult and alien when dealing with their young children. In her book *A Natural History of Love* Diane Ackerman (1994: 5) notes the difficulties we experience in expressing love:

> As a society we are embarrassed by love. We treat it as if it were an obscenity. We are reluctant to admit to it. Even saying the word makes us stumble and blush. Why should we be ashamed of an emotion so beautiful and natural? Love is the most important thing in our lives, a passion for which we would fight or die, and yet we're reluctant to linger over its name.

As we explored this difficulty with the group, we came to realise that this was largely due to the fact that the women's own childhood experiences had been lacking in warmth and affection. They had gone on to enter relationships with partners who had also deprived them of positive experiences and warmth. The assertiveness training course quickly evolved into a 'Stroke City' event and the women were soon reporting more loving feelings and behaviours towards their children and finding more appropriate ways of dealing with their children's behaviours.

Sam – stroking for change

'Sam', was a young boy who came to me for weekly therapy sessions some years ago. We worked together for about a year. His early years were emotionally and physically abusive which resulted in him being removed from his parent's care by social workers. He had been in a number foster homes and children's homes where he had 'acted out' his distress and consequently been rejected and 'moved on' many times. He was referred to me by his carers, who were having difficulty with his behaviour at home and who explained that he had been excluded from school several times. He had been banned from Cubs, the local football team and his friends' parents would not allow their children to play with him. He was eight years old. His behaviours included hitting people, 'trashing' his room, swearing at teachers and other children, refusing to respond to simple, reasonable requests and a host of other behaviours, which elicited negative responses from others. Sam's 'stroke hunger' would seem to be more appropriately named 'stroke starved' (Steiner, 1974).

Important recent research by the Mental Health Foundation (1999) into the needs of children in the care system has focussed on the concept of resilience. One of the indicators of 'growing resilient children' was their ability to elicit positive responses from the adults looking after them (*ibid*.: 19). While Sam was a spirited and bright little boy; he had not found a way of getting people to like him. My treatment plan was then to work on stroking him for *being him – just as he was*, at the same time *stroking for change*, inviting him into behaviours which elicited positive strokes from others. Sam would arrive to a warm greeting "Hi, I've been looking forward to seeing you". (Only if I had – occasionally my work with Sam could be very hard). I would listen very carefully to everything he said, responding in an interested and loving way. These were positive unconditional strokes, which, having been brought up on a diet of negativity were sometimes difficult for him to accept. Children act out what they can't talk out and I would take a curious interest in his 'acting out' behaviours and explore with him the meaning of them for him. "So the teacher spoke to you in that tone you don't like and you stormed out of the class. Did that help you to feel better?"

My stroking for behaviour change would always be worded in the positive. I would never say "Thank you for not trashing my room today" rather; "I really like the way you treated the room today and the way you helped me put things away. Thanks". If he reported a good day at school I might say "Oh, so you talked politely to the teachers and had fun with the other children. It sounds like that worked well for you." One day he arrived and said "Barbara, can you help me to stop swearing?" I replied "What does it feel like when you swear at people". He replied that he felt like he was the boss and that people couldn't hurt him. I then enquired "Well if it makes you feel so good, why do you want to stop?" He thought for a moment and then replied "Well, it feels good just for one minute, and then people don't like me and I don't feel good then". Being in charge of his own therapy goals allowed Sam to engage with behavioural work with me in some of his subsequent sessions.

Over time, in an atmosphere of thoughtful stroking, Sam became able to accept positive strokes when they were offered. This was confirmed one day when he was occupied with some clay work and I said something kind to him. He laughed, and not looking up from his work said "Uh, you think I'm the king of the world don't you?" Some people find it very difficult to accept positive strokes, particularly when they have been brought up on a diet of negativity. Gladfelter (1977: 412), in his work on effective stroking suggests that "it is important in learning effective stroking to be able to decline the discounts that the patient gives in response to strokes". He suggests that potent stroking is dependent on the care with which words are linked together to become a stroke and that we should stroke carefully and specifically.

Sam also found ways of eliciting positive strokes from me. He would say things like "Do you like me" to which the response was always positive (and genuine). He was able to give positive strokes to me and to his carers. I modelled refusing strokes that I did not want "I don't want you to speak to me like that, Sam". This was an important one for Sam. It enabled him to do the same to other people if they were unkind to him. Gradually he was becoming more settled at school as he learned how to elicit positive responses from people. He began to 'bask' in the comfort of acceptance from his teachers and others around him. His negative behaviours reduced dramatically. Of course, other important work was being done with Sam at the same time as his therapy, and the love and support of his carers and other adults helped him to accept himself and others to accept him.

Conclusion

It is important in our work with children to model giving and accepting strokes. I teach it to student counsellors who I am involved in training. I encourage boasting and bragging in a fun way to desensitise people in confronting their fears of going against the stroke economy rules. I also model accepting positive strokes and refusing strokes that I don't want. I believe that the free exchange of strokes in all it's simplicity, is a most life-enhancing phenomenon for physical and psychological well-being of all people, but most significantly for those young people who are still waiting for love and acceptance by the adults around them.

References

Ackerman, D. (1994). *A natural history of love*. New York: Vintage.

Berne, E. (1961). *Transactional analysis in psychotherapy*. New York: Random House.

Berne, P.N., & Savary, L.M. (2000). *Building self-esteem in children*. New York: Crossroad.

Clarkson, P. (1992). *Transactional analysis psychotherapy: An integrated approach*. London: Routledge.

Emler, N. (2001). *Self-esteem: The costs and causes of low-self worth*. York: Joseph Rowntree Foundation.

Gladfelter, J. (1977). *Transactional analysis after Eric Berne*. New York: Harpers College Press.

Mental Health Foundation (1999). The big picture: Promoting children and young people's mental health needs. *Community Care*, 13–19 May: 18–20.

Mruk, C. (1999). *Self-esteem: Research, theory and practice*. London: Free Association Books.

Rogers, C. R. (1951). *Client-centered therapy*. Boston: Hougton Miffin.

Steiner, C. (1974). *Scripts people live*. New York: Grove Press.

Steiner, C. (2000). *The meming of love; Invention of the human heart*. Keynote lecture at the 3rd Adolescence Health Conference at the Royal College of Physicians in London, October 2000. www.claudesteiner.com.

Author Biography

Barbara Smith is a UKCP registered psychotherapist working as a Lecturer in Counselling and Social Work in Liverpool. She also has a private psychotherapy practice, specialising in Transactional Analysis with adults and children in individual and group psychotherapy. She has a strong research interest in anti-discrimination and oppression, and recently co-edited a book titled Anti-discriminatory Counselling Practice (Sage Publications). She is currently in the Maldives for two years, with VSO, where she will be setting up a counselling training course on the capital Island of Male. She will design and deliver a course in counselling for work with children, the first of its kind in the Maldives.

Self-esteem:

theory-driven practice

Peter Bunyan

Introduction

There has always been tension between academic theory and practice and subsequently, a suspicious relationship between members of the academic community and practitioners working in the facilitation of personal development in the outdoors. Whilst it is not the place of this piece to explore the authenticity of this relationship, it is written from a perspective that there needs to be a clear dialogue between both parties if, as professionals, we are to move forward in a meaningful way with a common language, purpose and understanding. As Henderson and Bialeschki (1989: 88) comment in relation to Outdoor Education, "it is commonly acknowledged that by strengthening the information exchange between various components of the outdoor education profession, better programs can be delivered to satisfy participants".

The development of theory-driven practice in relation to self-esteem requires both parties – theorists and practitioners – to be more respectful of each other. They need to work openly, collectively recognising the contribution that each can make to the future of our interaction with individuals – young and old. One of the problems that faces us as a profession is an acceptance of common terms. Perhaps our understanding of terms has been hampered by our unwillingness to adhere to those terms that are meaningful from the myriad of ones available.

Campbell (1984) notes the significance of self-esteem as a phenomenon. He highlights how, "a variety of thinkers, starting from different ideologies and backgrounds, have come to the conclusion that the self-esteem motive can explain virtually every facet of human behaviours" (*ibid.*: pxiii). As a result of this conclusion a variety of definitions has been developed to understand this phenomenon more fully. Three common definitions of self-esteem and associated theories are discussed here.

These not only provide an initial working platform for considering how theory drives practice, they also indicate how we might obtain a more meaningful understanding of self-esteem and enable greater dialogue between theorists and practitioners.

Defining self-esteem: three perspectives

1. Self-description and emotion

Fox (1990) differentiates between the term 'self-concept' (a series of statements which provide a self-description, e.g., I have brown hair and blue eyes) and 'self-esteem' (the evaluative judgements we attach to our self-description). Campbell and Lavallee (1993) term these the 'knowledge' and 'evaluative' components of self, the former comprising self-relevant information based on past experiences, the latter a self-reflexive attitude towards the self as an object. This partitioning of description and emotion is very simplistic; it would be difficult to conceive of a person viewing their self-description without it evoking some kind of associated emotion.

Individuals place different amounts of importance on the various parts of their self-esteem. Subsequently, this provides a motivation force directing their behaviour towards things that will reinforce their feelings of self-worth and to move away from things that will undermine it. This indicates that understanding self-esteem and its development must be viewed from an individual rather than a group perspective. If we fail to identify those aspects of an individual's self-esteem that are most salient to them, then our efforts to increase the positive way an individual views themself will be little more than haphazard.

Protecting self-worth

Having identified the need for individuals to feel good about themselves through maintaining high levels of self-esteem, we all frequently encounter situations where our self-esteem is vulnerable through not meeting the expectations of either ourselves or significant others. Thompson (1999: 5) highlights how, as human beings, we all enjoy success:

> Everyone loves to succeed; no-one likes to fail. I dare say all of us have at least one experience of monumental failure… yet the memory haunts us. We joke about it but cringe inwardly. The memory remains crisp even after the emotion has faded.

Here self-esteem and sensation-seeking are inextricably linked. An individual's self-esteem sits on a delicate knife-edge of perceived success or perceived failure as they participate in risk-taking activities, such as outdoor pursuits. Perceived successful new encounters enhance self-esteem and perceived unsuccessful ones potentially reduce levels of self-esteem and subsequent self-worth. Thompson (*ibid.*: 8) recognises that, for some, failure brings extreme anxiety leading to an internalisation of global self-doubt. He identifies five characteristic behaviours that might signify to facilitators that individuals are exposing themselves to potential self-worth damage.

1. Self-worth protection.
2. Self-handicapping.
3. Procrastination.
4. Defensive pessimism.
5. Impostor fears.

The first of these – self-worth protection – describes a strategy whereby an individual withdraws effort thereby avoiding subsequent failure and emotive consequence. Prolonged utilisation of this strategy results in inconsistent performance and a recognisable reluctance to engage in group activities. The second protection strategy – self handicapping – is recognised by individuals verbalising prior to performance a handicap such as an injury, nullifying the effect of any failure, and making more significant success despite the handicap. The third strategy – procrastination – is characterised by the individual setting unrealistic targets and demands of themselves. Inevitable failure then becomes an acceptable norm with greatly diminished self-esteem consequences. The fourth self-esteem protection mechanism – defensive pessimism – is the exact reverse. Individuals sacrifice self-esteem enhancement in favour of self-esteem preservation by deliberately setting low targets and demands.

As a consequence, self-esteem status quo is maintained to the detriment of increased levels of self-worth. The final mechanism – impostor fears – centres more on the handling of the positive emotions that accompany successful encounters. Individuals with low levels of self-esteem generally prefer to maintain their existing level of self-esteem, albeit low, rather than to take on board higher levels of esteem that may later give rise to heightened anxiety through increased expectation. Typically, these individuals attribute success to luck or to other individuals. Thompson (1999) again underlines the need for under-standing self-esteem and its development to be viewed on an individual rather than group basis, and for us to have specific knowledge of our clients, without which there is little chance of unlocking the potential of developmental facilitation.

2. Dissonance and self-esteem

James (1890) provides a second classical definition of self-esteem. He introduces the notion of dissonance; our self-esteem being the emotions attached to the difference between our successes and what we aspire of ourselves: self-esteem = success.

Pretensions

The complex processes of maintaining self-esteem are evident by the way in which individuals attribute success and failure to themselves. Thompson (1999) proposes that the level of 'evaluative threat' will play a part in determining whether an individual attributes a negative outcome to him or herself or an external event. As he points out "evaluative threat is unlikely to occur where threat to self-esteem is softened by circumstances which enable a negative outcome to be explained by a factor which is unrelated to ability" (*ibid.*: 102). In situations of high evaluative threat, individuals are likely to invoke the protection mechanisms outlined above.

In creating a non-evaluative environment facilitators should consider three time spans that are typically termed 'pre-impact, impact and post-impact' (Mosston and Ashworth, 1986). Prior to facilitation (pre-impact) trainers should be aware that previous history of failure in the activity or similar activities, along with encountering new activities with uncertain outcomes, gives rise to high evaluative threats. Through 'normative grading practices' (Thompson, 1999) – individuals comparing themselves with others or through facilitators basing their feedback on collective performances – similar effects occur during the impact phase. Finally, 'non contingent evaluative feedback' (*ibid.*) should be avoided; this is where knowledge of performance is given in a non-constructive or specific way. For example, saying to someone "you were good" introduces uncertainty of reward; the participant is provided with nothing constructive that future performances can be based on. Global group feedback attaches the same comments to a variety of performances. Again, this inconsistency leaves the individual questioning the level and appropriateness of their own performance. Under such conditions action has little effect on self-esteem. The definition given by James (1890) also highlights the importance of accurate and appropriate target-setting (pretensions), and the need for facilitators to have a working knowledge of appropriate target setting strategies, such as SMARTER[1] principles, and the mechanisms that are used to formulate an image of the 'ideal self'.

3. Mirror self-images

Jacobson (1964) provides the third definition of self-esteem. She states that "it is the degree we are able to live up to our wishful concept of self, the degree that we are omnipotent" (*ibid.*: 6). Again the notion of dissonance put forward by James (1890) is reinforced, but it is placed in the context of being 'all important' and in control of our own destiny. He further comments that, due to their gregarious nature, humans have a desire to be noticed in a favourable way by their fellow humankind.

Coopersmith (1967) establishes that knowledge of our self-competence is arrived at through two sources. The first of these is 'self-dependent sources'; self-perceptions derived independent of others. The second 'other dependent sources' are built upon the interactions we have with significant others in our lives and include notions of 'acceptance', 'praise', 'friendship', 'love' and 'respect'. Thus there are as many extensions to our self-esteem as there are people who hold past and present reflective images of us (Mead, 1934; Coopersmith, 1967;

Woodman, 1973). As pointed out by Baumeister *et al.* (1999: 248), the 'mirror' self images of significant others are potentially the most influential on our self-esteem:

> When favourable views of self are confronted with unflattering external feedback, the person faces a choice point. The affective response will depend on the path chosen. One path is to accept the external appraisal and to revise one's self-esteem in a downward direction. Sadness, anxiety, and dejection might well result from such a course. In contrast, the other path is to reject the external appraisal and uphold one's more favourable self-appraisal.

It is argued by Rosenberg (1979) that the decision to accept or reject external feedback is based on two related criteria. Firstly, how 'valued' is it; does it conform to any degree of consensus, and has someone who is most like our own self-perception given it? (Backman *et al.*, 1963). Secondly, is it credible; has somebody who is 'role specific' and, therefore, considered expert and significant given it? Equally, has it been given by an 'orientational significant' other whose opinion is respected in a variety of contexts? (Denzin, 1966).

Principally, our parents, when we are young, and our teachers and peers as we grow older, are the key-holders to our self-esteem development; their views are the most valued and influential. Faced with the perception of adverse feedback it is likely that individuals' recourse to the self-worth protection strategies, as outlined earlier, will come into action. Self-esteem has, therefore, both trait and state characteristics (Rosenberg, 1979; Mortimer *et al.*, 1982). These characteristics, therefore, add more complexity to any notion of understanding levels of self-esteem, or promoting its development. This puts into perspective the potential we have as facilitators, even more so when the issue of selective importance is considered. What veridical value might an individual place on an activity that is unimportant to them, that takes place in the company of individuals who they value very little, and is facilitated by a person who is unknown to them in terms of intention, trustworthiness and sincerity?

Conclusion

As facilitators, one of the most important points we must recognise is that a person's self-esteem is resilient to change (Lawrence, 1996). This is advantageous in terms of damage limitation, but underlines once more the difficulties that are encountered developmentally. The phrase, "meaningful experiences, plenty and often" (Lawrence, 1999: 54) is a good adage to guide our practice. This highlights the need to approach self-esteem development from an individual rather than a group perspective, and for interactions to be based on experiences that are significant to the participant rather than to the facilitator. The state and trait dimensions of self-esteem identify the potential problems that might be encountered when individuals are taken to unknown surroundings, placed in unfamiliar groups and then subsequently return to their home environment. In the United Kingdom, for example, consideration needs to be given to the 'City Bound Model' of Outdoor Education outlined by Barrett and Greenaway (1995), whereby the role of providing outdoor developmental experiences in a more familiar, urban environment is recognised.

Anyone seriously doing more than lip service to the development of self-esteem should also become acquainted with some of the hierarchical models that have attempted to map out the concept (e.g., Fox, 1990; Shavelson & Bolus, 1982). These models are illustrative of why there is a need for plentiful experiences and why one-off activities have minimal effect on the lower sub-domains of self-esteem (e.g., physical or academic worth) and no effect on global self-esteem (e.g., how we generally value ourselves).

We owe it to our clients, our profession and ourselves to deepen our understanding of the development of self-esteem. It is a fundamental psychological trait that has entered everyday language. How many songs can you name with self-esteem in the words? We as facilitators need to move beyond the words of Michael Jackson (*Keep the Faith*: "...all you need is the will to want it, and uhh a little self-esteem."), Shania Twain (*Black Eyes, Blue Tears*: "Finally found my self-esteem. Finally I'm forever free to dream."), and Savage Garden (*Affirmation*: "I believe that beauty magazines promote low self-esteem.") if we are to attain the development of self-esteem as an outcome of our encounters with individuals.

Endnote

1. SMARTER (Specific, Measurable, Attainable, Realistic, Time Phased, Evaluated, Recorded) is a principle developed by the National Coaching Foundation to guide goal setting primarily by athletes and coaches. See Crisfield, P. (1993). *Planning your programme: A home study pack*. Leeds: National Coaching Foundation.

References

Backman, C. W., Secord, P. F., & Pierce, J. R. (1963). The effect of perceived liking on interpersonal attraction. *Sociometry*, 26: 102-111.

Barrett, J., & Greenaway, R. (1995). *Why adventure? The role and value of outdoor adventure in young people and personal and social development. A review of research*. Coventry: Foundation for Outdoor Adventure.

Baumeister, R. F., Smart, L., & Boden, J. M. (1999). Relation of threatened egotism to violence and aggression: The dark side of self-esteem. In R, F. Baumeister (Ed.), *The self in social psychology* (pp. 240-280). Cleveland, Ohio: Psychology Press.

Campbell, J. D., & Lavallee, L. F. (1993). Who am I? The role of self-concept confusion in understanding the behaviour of people with low self-esteem. In R. F. Baumeister (Ed.), *Self-esteem. The puzzle of low self-regard* (pp. 3-20). New York: Plenum Press.

Campbell, R. N. (1984). *New science*. Boston: University of America Press.

Coopersmith, S. (1967). *The antecedents of self-esteem*. San Francisco: Freeman and Co.

Cournoyer, D. E., & Walds, C. K. (2000). *Research methods for social work*. Boston: Allyn and Bacon.

Denzin, N. K. (1966). The significant others of a college population. *Sociological Quarterly*, 7: 298-310.

Fox, K. R., (Ed.). (1990). *The complexities of self-esteem promotion in physical education and sport*. London: E & FN Spon.

Henderson, K. A., & Bialeschki, M. D. (1989). Outdoor Education Practitioners and Researchers: Working Together a Dialogue. *JOPERD*, April: 88-90.

Jacobson, E. (1964). *The self and the object world*. New York: International Universities Press.

James, W. (1890). *The principles of psychology*. New York: Holt.

Lawrence, D. (1996). *Enhancing self-esteem in the classroom*. London: Paul Chapman Publishing Ltd.

Mead, G. H. (1934). *Mind, self and society*. Chicago: University of Chicago Press.
Mortimer, J. T., Finch, M. D., & Kumka, D. (1982). Persistence and change in development: The multidimensional self-concept. In P. B. Baltes, and O. G. Brim (Eds.), *Life span development and behaviour* (pp. 263-313). Orlando, Florida: Academic Press.
Mosston, M., & Ashworth, S. (1986). *Teaching physical education*. Columbus, Ohio: Merrill Publishing Company.
Rosenberg, M. (1979). *Conceiving the Self*. New York: Basic Books.
Shavelson, R. J., & Bolus, R. (1982). Self-concept: The interplay of theory and methods. *Journal of Educational Psychology*, 74: 3-17.
Thompson, T. (1999). *Underachieving to protect self-worth: Theory, research and interventions*. Aldershot, Hampshire: Ashgate.
Woodman, L. (1973). *Perspectives of self-awareness*. Columbus, Ohio: Charles, E, Merrill Publishing Company.

Author Biography

Peter Bunyan is a Senior Lecturer in Adventure Education at University College Chichester. After completing his undergraduate studies at Exeter he taught for eight years in the Eastern Counties before returning to Exeter to run the Post-graduate Outdoor Education Programme, and undertake higher degree studies. After moving to Chichester he initiated the BA (Hons) Adventure Education degree, and is now working towards his PhD in the area of self-esteem development through adventure.

Self-esteem and relational voices: eating disorder interventions for young women in the outdoors

Kaye Richards

Introduction

Interventions in the outdoors aimed at assisting the personal development of young people frequently lead to an assumption that self-esteem enhancement is a beneficial outcome. For example, the Department for Education and Skills (2000:8) states that an objective for individuals participating in the Summer Activities Initiative for 16-Year Olds (now called the 'u-Project') includes "increasing confidence and self-esteem". This makes an assumption that such an increase will be achieved through participation in outdoor activities. After adopting a similar view as an outdoor educator and teacher I have, however, found myself in something of a paradoxical position. On the one hand, my work in the outdoors has been founded on such an assumption, yet in developing my work I have in fact started to question the very basis of this assumption. Research and practice working with a client group that has at its core a low self-esteem – that is women with eating disorders – have fuelled this questioning.

In examining the emphasis in psychology of an independent self – that is a personality that is driven towards self-sufficiency – the question is posed as to whether this reflects a dominant view. As a result, approaches to esteeming the self may fall short of what may be required in some intervention work for young people. Thus, in continuing the debate on the causes and costs of low self-worth there is a need to consider how current notions of the self are viewed, along with evaluating how understandings of the self are reflected in personal development practices. The linking of theory, research and practice in the intervention of eating disorders for young women in the outdoors will illustrate this need.

Eating disorders, self-esteem and young women

Early literature that examines the causes of eating disorders alludes to how a deficient sense of self is a key factor in its development (Bruch, 1973). As a result of not feeling good about oneself an individual, usually a young woman, turns to food control and pursues a low body weight as a way of reversing these negative feelings. Whether it is self-starvation with anorexia nervosa or bingeing and purging with bulimia nervosa, troubled eating becomes a key strategy for maintaining a self-esteem that has become fragile and at risk of collapse. Yet, this search for self-esteem is in many ways futile. Feelings of self-hate are only momentarily accompanied with feelings of self-like when food is controlled or body weight reduced. Further, as 80% of women diet to lose weight (Brown, 1993), for many women, irrespective of whether they are classified as having an 'eating disorder' or not, their sense of self and, hence, self-esteem is correlated to how good they feel about their bodies. As Button (1994: 18) points out, a factor in the prevention of eating disorders is a high self-esteem because body dissatisfaction is linked to a low self-esteem.

Wider influences upon young people's self-esteem

As the societal pressure for the 'pursuit of thinness' impacts on how young women feel about their bodies, a number of questions can be posed about the role of any individual's social environment in the formation of self-esteem. For example, how do social relationships and power relationships serve to impact upon how a person experiences and defines his or her individual self-esteem, and how is self-creation impinged upon? How might parts of the self for some young people become denied, thus limiting opportunities to 'feel' esteemed? What social groupings currently benefit from the dominant understandings of self-esteem and could it be that our current understandings in fact serve to perpetuate the low self-esteem of some of the groups we aim to target in our work? As pointed out by Ellis (1998: 253) having low self-esteem is often perceived as "deficient" and risks "pathologizing whole groups of individuals, without considering the possibility that these groups may actually conceptualise self-esteem differently from researchers and practitioners". Thus, the processes of developing and maintaining a high level of self-esteem need to be situated within a wider analysis of social and cultural process and circumstances. For example, if the symptoms of low self-esteem as expressed by young women with eating disorders are to be tackled, then the social construct of women's bodies in relation to women's psychological selves become an essential feature of any intervention strategy.

Examining links such as those above exemplify the complexity of the relationship between theory and practice in providing interventions for self-esteem enhancement. Yet, the linking of theory to practice is essential if the task of raising self-esteem is to be achieved. As Emler (2001: 60) points out, "programmes with a good grounding in theory and/or relevant research evidence consistently emerge as more effective". Interestingly, in actively linking theory, research and practice in the intervention of eating disorders, dominant understandings that underpin aspects of western psychology and thinking on self development come into question.

Self-esteem and eating disorders: a relational perspective

Emler tentatively refers to the significance of 'being in relation' in terms of achieving a high level of self-esteem. He suggests that the "quality of close relationships with others does appear to be a significant determinate of self-esteem – the likelihood of forming these relationships is itself a function of self-esteem" (*ibid.*: 60). After a closer examination of the developmental processes of disordered eating, the notion of 'being in relation' proves significant. Sesan and Katzman (1998: 81) highlight how the transitions faced by young women during adolescence serve to encourage a relational denial, which is a factor in the high rate of disordered eating symptomatic of adolescent girls.

> Eating disorder pathology develops as a response to the confusion and 'crisis of connection' that girls experience around the loss of their relational world, as they come of age within a culture that does not value these types of connections with others.

Relational psychology

Relational psychology takes the significance of relationship-building and maintenance as key to developing self-esteem. It is an approach to psychology that hinges upon ideas such as relational confidence and relational flexibility. An ability to attain and be able to sustain healthy relational contact and movement with others is central to an individual's internal valuing processes (Jordon, 1994). 'Being' and 'staying' in a relationship become essential to feeling good about oneself. Expression and development of one's relational capacity with others is essential to feeling esteemed. As stated by Jordon (*ibid.*) situations that create poor self-esteem are in fact characterised by "relational non-responsiveness". Thus what might commonly be termed as interdependent behaviour may, in fact, be the expression of a relational self-structure. That is, an individual is expressing a motivational tendency that leads towards healthy development. The relevance of this to the development of self-esteem is that if an individual experiences barriers and resistance from others that deny this relational capacity – i.e. feeling "unable to reach, touch, or affect the other person" – this can lead to "isolation, paralysis and self-doubt or self-blame" (*ibid.*: 3). Thus, in contrast to an autonomous view of the self, relational psychology highlights how the very nature of interdependent behaviour is seen as providing a core to the maintenance of self-esteem (Jordon *et al.*, 1991). As a result, the notion of 'growth in relational connection' becomes a central feature to raising and sustaining self-esteem.

Mastery, self-definition, separation from others, and independence are still commonly pursued and are highly prized goals in personal development. This raises the question of how appropriate the developmental aims of increasing self-sufficiency and individual autonomy actually are. Do such aims deny the necessary development of relational functions that would enable a more sustainable sense of self-worth? Consider, for example, why we strive for an independent self and in what ways interdependent behaviour is seen as negative, and at times even labelled as pathological?

Hearing relational voices

Many societal conditions risk discounting the importance of relational expression and the mechanisms of a relational self-structure. Emotionality and sensitivity, central facets of relational confidence, are often portrayed as a weakness and devalued as a female trait. In turn, these circumstances make women, in particular adolescent girls, vulnerable to the maintenance of a low self-esteem: a key process that enables them to sustain feelings of self-worth becomes impinged upon. A questioning and dislike of the self is then easily misplaced internally with the emergence of coping strategies through a dislike of one's body and troubled eating behaviours. Women use control of food and body as a way of feeling 'good' about themselves. It becomes an alternative to relational expression. Thus, troubled eating can be seen as a metaphor for finding it difficult to access relational voices: troubled eating masks troubled relationships. A reliance upon a low body weight and controlling eating creates a false sense of self-esteem. These behaviours then risk permeating women's psyche for much of their adult life. What is often used as a humorous statement – 'does my bum look big in this' – represents the prominence and acceptance of this discourse for women.

It is evident then that the emotional and psychological costs of relational denial – i.e. troubled relationships – lie at the core of many women's ongoing battle with feeling insecure, undervalued and negative about themselves. Low self-esteem as expressed by disordered eating can be seen as a response to societal conditions. This is, in part, a result of the devaluing of a relational self in an individualistic society (Surrey, 1984: Sesan & Katzman, 1998), whereby the feelings attached to relational denial are interwoven with the social discourse of women's bodies. Thus, in order to consider how to approach practical intervention work for disordered eating, it is important to view eating disorders as a form of troubled relationships expressed through troubled eating.

Women and eating disorders: reconnecting to a relational self in the outdoors

In developing an intervention to address disordered eating for women, de-emphasising food intake becomes a goal for personal change. Thus, rather than dealing with the response of not eating, the underlying devaluing system of a relational self needs to be reassessed. Yet, in examining the traditional ways of viewing the self in the outdoors, it becomes evident that the historical basis of outdoor adventure is steeped in 'relational denial'. This is because self-esteem enhancement in the outdoors has traditionally been based upon self-esteem being raised through achievement. In developing a relational approach to increasing self-esteem it becomes easily recognised that an intervention based

LIVERPOOL JOHN MOORES UNIVERSITY
LEARNING SERVICES

merely on achievement is fundamentally flawed. Feeling good about oneself after completing an outdoor activity may be only a temporary fix of self-esteem, whereby the underlying self-structure remains unaffected and low self-esteem remains fully intact.

In providing an outdoor development-based approach that is responsive to the needs of women with eating disorders, there is a need to examine the mechanisms by which the developmental functions of eating disorders interplay with an outdoor setting. Such an examination reveals how models of developing the self and, hence self-esteem enhancement, may in fact reinforce some of the developmental features of eating disorders. For example, common symptoms of disordered eating include control and mastery over the body, and a continual desire to work towards self-perfection and achievement. Yet, these remain inherent in the models of personal development commonly applied within the outdoors. The notion of 'overcoming fear' rather than 'listening to fear', and 'challenging the physical body' rather than 'nurturing the physical body' are commonplace. These aspects of the experience are significant for women with eating disorders, as both a denial of their fears and control of mind over body pivot around the core construction of a sense of self-esteem.

Perception of self-worth will play a part in how an individual takes meaning from an experience. For example, consider a common activity used – a trust fall. This activity immediately creates a space in which it heightens an individual's experience of their body weight and whereby physical identity becomes central to the activity. As women with eating disorders have accentuated fears in such areas, perhaps a more appropriate term for the activity would be a 'body fall'. This moves away from simply thinking that completing a trust fall will generate a positive experience. Instead, it invites us to ask how the psychological processes relevant to an individual's self-structure can be worked with to increase the likelihood of having a positive psychological impact upon a person's self-worth. This is not to say that this will be immediate. In the case of eating disorders, over-identification of the self with the body, along with the associated feelings attached to this self-structure, need to be worked with over a long period of time. However, when facilitated appropriately, an activity such as a 'body' fall may enable the psychological functions that maintain a low sense of self-worth to be challenged, supporting a more sustained process of change.

In evaluating the impact of an outdoor therapeutic-based intervention for women with eating disorders that took the above issues into account, it is worth considering one woman's experience in comparison to other counselling approaches she had previously experienced:

> Something changed with me ... I think really the situation I am in at the moment is having an understanding that I've tried to deny in the past, and rather than it being troubled eating it's troubled relationships.

Is this woman accessing and expressing her relational voice? Is there a link between a relational self-structure and disordered eating? What does this serve in her recovery from an eating disorder? Does this reconnection enhance what is commonly determined as low self-esteem? In many ways I suspect it does. However, in achieving such a connection there was no 'one-stop-shop' for personal development, nor was there one self–esteem inventory that could measure such change. What was required was a questioning of the models that propose particular views to individual change, coupled with a willingness to change practice, and also to align theory with practice. This highlights the complexity of developing strategies to develop self-esteem. As argued by Emler (2001: 60) a more thorough understanding of how one understands the processes of change and the meaning of self-esteem is required:

> The message is that a well-founded understanding of the phenomena one is trying to change will produce more effective efforts than facile intuitions of the 'positive feedback – good; negative feedback – bad' variety that permeate the self-esteem industry.

Accessing and developing relational voices of young people

Although goals of developing social relationships – which may be interpreted as relational psychology – are evident in youth development practices, these are not necessarily based upon a relational view of the self. Practice, in many ways, is still geared towards developing effective communication and peer relationships, to enhance an individual's capacity to achieve in a western world of being independent, self-sufficient and in pursuing self-perfection. By recognising that these processes are deeply embedded by cultural and social practices, it becomes evident that there is no simple answer to positively impacting upon self-esteem.

A training perspective

In Emler's (2001) questioning of what works best in the processes of self-esteem enhancement, he highlights other factors that require greater examination. One of these is the training and experience of those delivering an intervention (Emler, 2001: 57). Here Emler is recognising that the 'theories in action' of self-esteem have an impact upon any process of change. Thus, from an outdoor activity perspective it again reminds us that it is not the activity alone that will enhance self-esteem. The approach taken to facilitate an experience is what will, in part, enable an individual to make meaning for themselves in the light of how they construct their own individual self-esteem. This highlights how, in developing a relational based approach to youth development, key skills and strategies for knowing how to access and develop 'relational voices' in relationships with young people is required. Such a process is a complex interaction of inter-personal and intra-personal skills. For example, what does it look like to demonstrate and coach others in the skills of relational flexibility and relational mutuality? The practices of relational therapy highlight the micro skills required to facilitate a relational process in action (*see* Baker Miller, 1988). Yet these skills are not solely the terrain of a therapist. Any theoretical model of self-esteem enhancement and personal growth requires fundamental key skills in order to put its theory into practice. This raises the question of how youth professionals are trained in the core skills of working to improve young people's self-esteem. If considering a relational model this requires a more extended training emphasis than is currently evident, in order to ensure that the transfer from theory to practice is achieved.

A research perspective

As demonstrated by Emler (2001) research into self-esteem underpins theory and guides practice. Thus, in youth development practices we have to also recognise how the strategies used in research may determine the perspectives that we take to self-esteem. If we adhere to the saying 'what we see depends mainly on what we look for' it could be posed that the scientific (positivist) approaches to understanding self-esteem that are prominent in Emler's research report fail to access many other significant meanings. The meanings attached to some self-esteem inventories bear little relevance to how self-esteem develops within different individuals. On reflection, my own experience of using the Rosenberg (1965) Self-esteem Scale in eating disorder research (*see* Richards *et al.*, 2001), although a research tool often commonly used, was unable to give detailed insight into the actual processes of changes in self-esteem. This is particularly evident in research based on a relational perspective, as the relational interaction between the researched and the researcher becomes a site of the construction and exposure of meanings of self-esteem. Brown and Gilligan (1992: 8) highlight this in their research that examined the psychological and relational development of adolescence girls.

> We predicted that it was the relational nature of our conversation with girls that was responsible for the effects we had observed – clinical improvement, developmental progress, a strengthening of voice in relationship.

Conclusion

In the development of working with young women with eating disorders, a shift is required from viewing self-esteem as being constructed as an individual trait into recognising the centrality of relationships beyond the self. This in itself provides a step towards embracing 'other' meanings of self-esteem, and challenges pathological views that are inherent in women's mental health, especially towards eating disorders. In accessing and understanding the processes of 'relational voices' of young people, the research agendas sought and research questions asked need to be developed further. This will require a move away from a search for proving what we think we know works, towards being prepared to explore alternative views and perspectives.

Developing models of prevention and intervention for an issue that still represents one of the highest mortality rates of all 'psychiatric illnesses' - anorexia nervosa – highlights how these debates on self-esteem are not futile: lives are at stake. This is perhaps even more significant today as we see the rates of disordered eating increasing. Further debate is needed, therefore, not only into what we might mean by self-esteem, but also into what this might mean for how we approach practice, the client groups we target, the skills we require as practitioners and how we view our own sense of self in relation to this issue. As we rethink our understandings, we inevitably risk exposing the inadequacies of how we currently construct and link theory and practice with our endeavours of self-esteem enhancement in action. However, this can only be of a positive benefit as it will provide a step forward in being able to feel more confident in knowing the why and the how in tackling the 'costs and causes of low self-worth'.

References

Baker Miller, J. (1988). *Connections, disconnections and violations*. Stone Center Colloquium Series, No. 33. MA: Wellesley College.

Brown, C. (1993). Feminist therapy: Power, ethics and control. In C. Brown & K. Jasper (Eds.), *Consuming passions: Feminist approaches to weight preoccupation and eating disorders* (pp.120-136). Toronto: Second Story Press.

Brown, L. M., & Gilligan, C. (1992). *Meeting at the crossroads. Women's psychology and girls' development.* London: Harvard University Press.

Burstow, B. (1992). *Radical feminist therapy. Working in the context of violence.* London: Sage Publications.

Brown, L. M., & Brodsky, A. M. (1992). The future of feminist therapy. *Psychotherapy*, 29 (1): 51-57.

Bruch, H. (1973). *Eating disorders: Obesity, anorexia nervosa and the person within.* New York: Basic Books.

DfEE (2000). *Invitation to Tender (ITT) for Summer Activities for 16 Year Olds – Pilot Programmes in 2001*. London: DfEE.

Ellis, S. J. (1998). Is self-esteem political? *Feminism and Psychology*, 8 (2): 251-256.

Emler, N. (2001). *Self-esteem. The costs and causes of low self-worth*. York: Joseph Rowntree Foundation / YPS.

Jordon, J. V. (1994). *A relational perspective to self-esteem*. Stone Center Colloquium Series, No. 70. MA: Wellesley College.

Jordon, J. V., Kaplan, A. G., Miller, J. B., Stiver, I. P., & Surrey, J. L. (1991). *Women's growth in connection. Writings from the Stone Center*. London: Guildford Press.

Richards, K., Peel, J. F. C., Smith, B., & Owen, V. (2001). *Adventure therapy and eating disorders. A feminist approach to research and practice*. Ambleside: Brathay Hall Trust.

Rosenberg, M. (1965). *Society and the adolescent self-image*. Princeton, NJ: Princeton University Press.

Sesan, R., & Katzman, M. (1998). Empowerment and the eating-disordered client. In I. Bruna Seu & M. Collen Heenan (Eds.), *Feminism and psychotherapy. Reflections on contemporary theories and practices* (pp. 78-95). London: Sage Publications.

Surrey, J. L. (1984). *Eating patterns as reflection of women's development*. Stone Center Colloquium Series, No. 9. MA: Wellesley College.

Author Biography

Kaye Richards is Research Leader at Brathay Hall Trust. She is also a Lecturer for post-graduate students in Development Training at St Martin's College, specialising in Adventure Therapy and Outdoor Education. Her PhD research has been the development of adventure therapy interventions for women with eating disorders. She has also been developing adventure therapy training and practices in the UK, is a member of the International Adventure Therapy Organisation and, amongst other outdoor texts, recently edited 'Therapy within Adventure'. She continues to pursue her interest in psycho-spiritual psychotherapy. (Email: kaye.richards@brathay.org.uk).

Brathay
inspiring people

At Brathay, our powerful approach to learning uses real experiences to help young people recognise their talents, achieve beyond their expectations, and to develop their personal qualities and social skills. We develop programmes that utilise adventurous activities, art and drama, and use a variety of reviewing techniques to draw learning from the experiences.

Tailor-made courses

Through a process of consultation with group leaders, we develop flexible training programmes that meet the needs of young people. Using a team of experienced staff, we deliver these programmes, either on our site or at off-site venues. Brathay's tailor-made courses complement and support the longer-term work of youth organisations and are regularly designed as an integral part of existing youth work programmes.

Solid Ground courses

Solid Ground is a five-day programme aimed at Year 9 students, delivered over three terms within school. Solid Ground challenges the behaviour of young people and explores choices, decisions and consequences. It effectively complements the PSHE and Citizenship curriculum.

Trainer Training

We work closely with youth organisations to provide tailor-made training for their staff. We also run accredited residential courses for individuals working with young people, and deliver modules of a Masters Degree in Development Training, in partnership with St. Martin's College.

Corporate work

At Brathay we believe that individuals are the key to organisational success. Our distinctive experience-based approach to behavioural change is internationally recognised and we work with a wide range of major companies, in areas such as organisational, leadership and team development. All profits generated from our corporate work benefit our work with young people.

Brathay Academy

The Brathay Academy builds on Brathay's expertise in experiential development training. It brings together research, theory and practice to create a centre of excellence in people development in the areas of education, youth work and management learning. As the Academy grows, it will provide a source of innovation and development, disseminating its findings in order to benefit the community.

Brathay youth publications

Occasional Papers

1 *Research from the Ground up: Post-Expedition Adjustment.* P. Allison, (2000).

2 *Adventure Therapy & Eating Disorders. A Feminist Approach to Research & Practice.* K. Richards, J. C. F. Peel, B. Smith, V. Owen, (2001).

Youth Development Papers

1 *Self-esteem and Youth Development.* K. Richards (Ed.), (2003).

Brathay corporate publications

Organisation Development Topical Papers

1 The future of work | Teams | The psychological contract | Teambuilding

2 Experiential learning |Managing knowledge | Facilitation | Corporate universities

3 Creative teams | Cartooning | Creativity, strategy and change | Strategic alignment

4 Emotional intelligence | Learning to feel | Emotional labour

5 HRM | Ego-states & scripts | Graduates into business | How transfer happens

6 Take me to your leader | Leadership & emotional acumen | Wise learners, wise leaders | Fundamentalism in strategy development | Working together

7 Feeling valued at work? | Valuing people | Engaging and inspiring people